Tears in the Desert

LESSONS FROM THE JOYS AND SORROWS OF GOD'S CALL

KARL H. HELLER, PhD

WESTBOW PRESS®
A DIVISION OF THOMAS NELSON & ZONDERVAN

WestBow Press books may be ordered through booksellers or by contacting:

WestBow Press
A Division of Thomas Nelson & Zondervan
1663 Liberty Drive
Bloomington, IN 47403
www.westbowpress.com
1 (866) 928-1240

ISBN: 978-1-9736-0263-7 (sc)
ISBN: 978-1-9736-0262-0 (hc)
ISBN: 978-1-9736-0264-4 (e)

Library of Congress Control Number: 2017914156

Print information available on the last page.

WestBow Press rev. date: 09/26/2017

CONTENTS

DEDICATION

IN LOVING MEMORY

This book is dedicated to Christian Anne, my first grand-daughter who was stillborn on December 31, 1979. There are no words that can express the feelings of loss and grief in my soul, but God laid on my heart the following thoughts based on His promises to quench my sorrow. They express His comfort to me about this precious little girl:

She never saw the light of day,
But God had planned her destiny,
Delivered from a world of tears,
It's now the voice of Christ she hears:
"My little one come unto to me,
I give you life eternally,"
And by His promise and my faith,
One day I'll see her face to face.

ACKNOWLEGDEMENTS

J.B. BLACKFORD, Editor

Even with the best writing skills every author needs the services of a knowledgeable and competent literary expert. Jennifer Blackford, better known as "Jen" made an outstanding contribution to this book with her untiring dedication and always ready advice. Her valuable insights into the contents, style, and arrangement of this work are greatly appreciated. Without her able assistance this book could not have been written.

WILLIAM R. JONES, Mentor, Author, Industrialist, Philanthropist, Founder and CEO of SOLAR ATMOSPHERES, INC.

It was my highly esteemed Christian friend and brother in the Christian faith, Bill Jones, who gave me the idea of writing this book. Throughout the writing process of this book he stood by me with valuable suggestions and encouragement and his truly extraordinary generosity made its publication possible. My heartfelt appreciation and gratitude for his magnanimous assistance are beyond words. May the Lord continue to bless this prominent Christian entrepreneur, his family, and his company with ongoing success, and his dedicated mission of helping build the kingdom of God on earth.

ENDORSEMENTS

DR. FRANK JAMES:
Karl Heller's new book, Tears in the Desert: Lessons from the Joys and Sorrows of God's Call, provides an up-close and personal account from the frontline of pastoral ministry. This is a refreshingly candid account of why pastoral ministry is so very challenging and at the same time so very important. By recounting the triumphs and tragedies of his own ministry, Dr. Heller is an able and wise guide, especially for seminarians preparing for pastoral ministry.

Frank A. James III, DPhil, PhD, President and Professor of Historical Theology, Biblical Theological Seminary, Philadelphia

REV. DR. JOHN CLARK
Tears in the Desert was a title that immediately intrigued me since, having served 40 some years in pastoral activities, I have shed a few tears myself. I was introduced to this book by a mutual friend whom I share with Dr. Heller, and I am very grateful. It reveals a unique and captivating look at a life of Christian service that is both inspiring and captivating.

Every Practical Theology department in schools training for the ministry should make use of this testimony of God's guidance and grace. Without fear of contradiction, I would affirm that it leaves nothing out by way of preparation. Serving in the neighborhood of two large seminaries and having taught briefly in another I have helped mentor and prepare many men and I would have been happy to have used this book with them.

I have never had the opportunity to meet Karl Heller, but there were many times in my ministry I would have benefited from his wise counsel. Now, thanks to his frank and moving testimony all of us can benefit and should. He deals with doctrinal problems in churches, family and marriage, discrimination, tent making, tragedy and funerals, stewardship of money and time, and a host of other subjects with which the average pastor must cope, and possibly shed tears in his part of the desert.

Rev. Dr. John P. Clark, honorably retired after 36 years as pastor of the Lansdale Presbyterian Church in America.

"In God's providence, an at-risk youth in Hitler's Germany was miraculously spared, and drawn to faith in Christ. Blessed with a theological education, his ministry took him worldwide enriching others through evangelistic zeal, love for Scripture and gifts of education. Now, the Rev. Dr. Karl Heller, at the end of his remarkable ministry, shares his fascinating and hard-won lessons on being a true pastor, a Seelsorger—one who cares for souls. His many wise insights encourage, inspire and edify. Although gleaned through tears of sorrow, he shows how by divine grace these pastoral truths yield tears of joy and streams in the desert. Pastors and congregants alike herein possess a guide for the cure of souls that just might cure their souls and sustain their work for Christ."
Dr. Peter A. Lillback, President Westminster Seminary, Philadelphia

PREFACE

There are those who consider one sentence in the Bible consisting of only two words as the most beautiful in all of Scripture: "Jesus wept" (John 11:35). That phrase is repeated also in Luke 19:41 and in Hebrews 5:7. Our Lord Jesus was deeply touched by human suffering, and His love for people was expressed in His tears of sadness. But I believe, although there is no Biblical record,that Jesus may also have wept when he experienced the deserts of apostasy, mockery, loneliness, injustice and the agony of excruciating mental and physical pain.

The tears Jesus shed, recorded and unrecorded, reveal not only His caring for a sinful humanity, but a humility in grandeur that sent a message: It is alright for His servants also to shed the tears of sadness, compassion as well as joy and peace as they embark upon their call of helping to build the kingdom of God. To put it another way, a pastoral ministry of empathy, passion for souls, and sensitivity to human suffering cannot happen without tears, but they ultimately also result in the tears of victory over sin, triumph over self, and a deep sense of happiness that only Christ can offer.

This book revolves around such a ministry during which I came to know both the tears of blessing and of bitterness. The objective of this book is to provide not just an interesting story packed with the emotions of challenge, fruitfulness and failure, but more importantly to convey the important lessons I learned from my service for the Lord.

Here I present a story that depicts my labors in a desert of lost and searching souls while trying to come to grips with my own sinfulness through which

God, in His mercy, strengthened and matured my faith as I sought to reach more and more people with the saving gospel of Jesus Christ. At times my office became a desert of loneliness after I closed the door behind me while the tears of compassion – and sometimes contrition – flowed during tragedies, after difficult funerals, and at times of personal mistakes and defiance when God seemed so far away. But, again, there were also tears of joy and gratitude when men and women declared their faith in Christ, and in the realization that our Heavenly Father understands us, forgives and enables us, and expects us never to give up on the task of building His kingdom on earth.

The peculiarity of this record of Christian service lies in the diversity of my ministry to people in different churches, denominations, religious and secular organizations with divers theological and ideological preferences scattered over four continents. My own epitaph for all those years of ministry is best expressed with the powerful reassurance from the Psalmist, "Those who sow in tears will reap with songs of joy," (Ps.126:5, NIV) and the Apostle John, who declares "Now the dwelling of God is with men, and he will live with them. They will be his people...and he will wipe away every tear from their eyes," (Rev. 21:4, NIV).

INTRODUCTION

After my graduation from high school, which in Germany and some other European countries is not unlike leaving a typical American Junior College in terms of academic standards, I studied economics and business administration in Hamburg. At the same time I also worked as a student intern for two large companies that were owned by the same family. The future seemed promising as a result of promotions and the prospect of a lucrative career in two major domestic industries which also offered exciting possibilities for international commerce.

But after my conversion to Christ in 1949 I developed a fervent desire to serve on a foreign mission field. With high level contacts in England, I was looking at East Africa (the former Tanganyika) as a possible destination. But my application for an entry visa was denied by the British authorities because East Africa had been a German colony before the end of World War II in 1945 and as a German citizen I was denied entry into that country.

In contrast to my interest in foreign mission service to reach the unsaved with the gospel of Christ, I felt no desire to continue my studies for a church ministry, although I was given the opportunity by a Christian industrialist from Blackpool, England, who offered to pay all of my seminar and living expenses if I decided to study for a church pastorate. However, I had not lost my desire to study at an accredited college for foreign missionary service.

Perhaps it was the fact that I had become disillusioned with institutionalized Christianity as a result of my experience with the theologically liberal (neo-orthodox) Lutheran Church in Germany. Although I had been baptized and confirmed in that Church, and engaged in lengthy Bible studies which I had found spiritually unproductive, I found Christ outside organized religion in a non-denominational Conference Center operated by the evangelical Torchbearer Ministry in England. I had also been involved in the evangelistic outreach of the Scottish All Male Voice Festival Choir while preparing myself for service on a foreign mission field with studies at the Bible Training Institute in Glasgow. I also served one summer with the Scottish Evangelistic Council doing colportage work (an itinerant ministry going from door to door and selling Christian books and Bibles) in Northern Scotland. During my studies I had the opportunity to preach in a number of churches in England, Scotland and Ireland, but always with an emphasis on evangelism. I had (wrongly) assumed that the work of a local pastor was boring and routine and unfulfilling in that one was preaching to the same "saved" people every Sunday and I saw no challenge in that. I had yet to discover the importance of a regular pastoral ministry and that even the people of faith need the regular teaching of God's Word that is essential for spiritual growth, personal edification and for the "Body of Christ" to survive in a sinful world.

Even beyond my negative feelings about becoming a minister of a church I harbored a nagging doubt about the role of a pastor. I saw his work as more of a moral advocate than that of an evangelist. Some of the churches I had visited resembled social clubs mostly designed for making the best of this world with hardly a reference to Christ's redemptive sacrifice for our eternal souls.

I was shaping the opinion that a church that fails to reach out to the community – and beyond that through foreign missions to the world – cannot grow and will eventually become stagnant and die.

Later in my ecclesiastical career I came to appreciate the pastor's major function as what the Germans call a "Caretaker of Souls" (Seelsorger). I realized that preaching and teaching the Word of God is only a part of a far more challenging ministry which labors toward the sanctification of those who have been justified by faith. I humbly submit that this is a solemn duty many pastors do not see as a priority.

But I also viewed the church ministry of a pastor in a more critical way. An illustration for this may be given from the military. We often sing "Onward Christian soldiers, marching as to war," but these soldiers had their own ideas about any "command structure." Imagine an Army officer, after lengthy training at a military academy, planning an attack on the enemy and drafting appropriate battle plans. But these plans had to be submitted to every lower ranking officer for approval. Human nature being what it is, one can imagine the ensuing diversity of opinions! Everybody would have his own ideas about how to proceed thereby impeding, if not nullifying, the whole idea of leadership and command. It would be unlikely that such a military force would ever get off the ground, let alone wage a victorious battle. This scenario in my mind was further aggravated by the fact that while the army officer was paid by his government, the pastor was paid by his "troops" – an unhealthy situation too flawed to produce the best leadership.

Well, there you have it! There is a basic incongruity in the organized church and the pastor as a "hireling." He may well be the most qualified spiritual leader of his congregation, but exercising that leadership according to divine intention is another matter. I saw the solution to the problem in a delicate balancing act between asserting my authority as a servant of God more with gentle persuasion than rigid insistence. In matters of doctrinal authority, I was the only trained theologian in the church and rarely encountered a church member or official who questioned that. At the same time I realized that there are many other aspects of church life, like church finance, building maintenance, and caring for the needy that were better carried out with the help of the church's ruling elders and deacons. A prayerful accord in thought and purpose for the congregation's major mission objectives between the pastor and church leadership help to optimize a clearer vision and achieve the priorities of a church's goals. The designation of "ruling elders" and "teaching elders" (pastors) in the Presbyterian denomination shows that all authority in the church must be shared, but at the same time it is vital to respect the different functions of the pastor and the elected elders and other church officers.

I must point out here that I am definitely not against the church and the pastorate. After all, I ended up being a pastor myself against my own inclinations. But I soon discovered that my ministry was most effective when I followed the example of the Apostle Paul who earned his living, at least for part of his ministry, as a "tent-maker." Yes, he actually made tents and sold them for a living so that he could pursue God's call to a vital ministry to the Christian communities of his day.

Of the thirteen churches or pastoral charges discussed in this book, I ministered in only five full-time. The other eight churches I served concurrent with other activities such as college teaching and business consulting. Pastorates in rural Canada usually consisted of several dispersed congregations with the main church located in a larger town or village. These smaller congregations are not part of the thirteen mentioned above and only commented on if they are the result of new church development or if I had significant learning experiences in those locations.

Most of my income during my 50 years of ministry came from college teaching, lectures and speeches to various organizations and other secular work. Despite the heavy burden of engaging in two or even three careers at one time, I felt more empowered and effective in the pulpits and lecterns in front of me than I might have felt if my income had depended on church offerings alone. Beneath all of these feelings about preaching the gospel was my deep conviction that God's Word of eternal salvation is not for sale and cannot be bought with money.

How then did it happen that, with all these doubts, I became involved in a lengthy and intensive church career? This is a long story presented here with only the highlights of my experiences and a focus on the lessons learned each time.

It all began while I was working at Three Counties Hospital (a mental institution) located in Arlesey, Bedfordshire, England. For foreigners like me holding only a student visa, the British Government granted special work permits for selective types of employment especially in areas where there was a shortage of labor, like helping patients with basic care in mental hospitals.

After working at the hospital for a year, the director of the facility told me that he had heard me preach at a local church and expressed his desire to visit with me at my home. During his visit he shared with me that he always wanted to become a pastor. His brother was a minister in the United Church of Canada and had suggested to him that he and his family move there and study for the ministry. The UCC was apparently looking for qualified men to become ministers in that denomination. But the gentleman's wife did not want to leave England because of very close family ties, so he reluctantly prayed that the Lord would lead him to somebody else to go in his place. He told me that after he had heard me preach at the Letchworth Baptist Church, God had impressed upon him in a vision that I was the person to go his place!

This development stunned me and was the last thing I had expected even as we had prayed for some time that God, having blocked my ambitions for East Africa, would direct us to another field of service. As my wife and I began praying to seek God's will, something strange happened.

I had developed a constant fever and an X-ray revealed a shadow on my left lung. In answer to my questions the doctor told me that I needed complete rest and, he joked, best of all "ninety-nine percent pure air." Where would I find such "pure air"? The doctor grinned, "well, one place I can think of are the Shetland Islands." Very amusing, indeed – the Shetlands were 240 miles NE of Scotland in the North Atlantic. They were remote, underdeveloped and sparsely populated. How could anyone want to live and work there? Well, with God anything is possible!

A week later I received a letter from the United Free Church of Scotland. I had preached in several of their churches while studying in Glasgow and they had apparently followed my progress. The letter contained a startling message: Would I be interested in serving as a lay missionary in one of their churches located on the Shetland Islands? Clearly, this was God's call that could not be denied. We left for the Shetlands three weeks later.

But then there was the invitation to go to Canada. Visa requirements mandated a medical examination and a chest X-ray. A shadow on the lung would mean denial. God simply provided the "ninety-nine percent" pure air that was to cure my ailment. But the move to the Shetland Islands also resulted in a worthwhile ministry among some of the most endearing people I have ever met. After a few months and another medical examination, the Canadian authorities in Aberdeen declared me "healthy and fit" for an immigration visa. And so it was that after serving the United Free Church of Baltasound for the better part of a year, we set out for the greatest adventure of our lives – beginning a new ministry in Canada. I wanted to be a missionary in a hot climate – Africa. God directed me to become a minister in a cold climate – Canada. As somebody once said, "Man proposes and God disposes."

CHAPTER ONE
The Early Beginnings

The somewhat hectic and diversified activities related in this book are scattered across ten countries, more than a dozen congregations and numerous organizations, so they are best understood with some context as to how they became the story of my life and ministry.

It all began at Capernwray Hall, a beautiful, castle-like Christian conference center in Northern England through the ministry of Major Ian Thomas, a popular British evangelist and director of the center. This was in early September, 1949, and I had just become a Christian. It was expected from new converts to Christ to give a public testimony to their newly found faith, and at a Christian Conference Center one had the best chance to do just that. And so I stood in front of a crowd of some 200 mostly young people who listened attentively to what I had to say – stumbling through my carefully prepared words meticulously crafted in English, which was not my native tongue. When I realized that such a style didn't work for me I threw caution to the wind and told the crowd in broken English what I felt in my heart: An exceeding sense of joy and peace I had never felt before.

This little speech, lasting less than five minutes, was the beginning of a speaking career that was to span more than half a century as God called me to teach and preach eventually on three continents. My second testimony was a bit easier and given in German to a small group of believers in Hamburg, my hometown, who gave me the warmest welcome as a new

Christian and all the encouragement I needed to move on while praying for divine guidance concerning my future.

After leaving behind a promising career in business and industry, I received my first grounding in the knowledge of His Word while attending an inter-denominational Bible School in England, followed by a short term of study in Switzerland. I finally enrolled in the more ambitious and formal studies of a two-year program of theology and missions in Glasgow, Scotland. What I learned there was to be the foundation of many years of formal studies at a Canadian seminary and three major universities. Throughout my studies in Britain, which were later supplemented by work in the medical sector, God called me to an itinerant ministry of public speaking and preaching that was to take me all over the British Isles, including Ireland. But different geographical locations were not the only interesting features of my ministry.

During my study days in Glasgow I participated in group evangelism with my fellow college students as we preached from street corners to long queues waiting to enter the cinema. They were waiting targets as a standing audience for evangelism. Also, in the so-called "lodging houses" located in the city, we preached the gospel to unfortunate men and women who had been harshly condemned as "the scum of society." In stark contrast to these activities I was being chauffeured on weekends in a luxury automobile called at the time a "Rolls Bentley" in the company of a wealthy industrialist and his family. This generous Christian man, Aldworth Cowan and his brother, John, were the owners of Scotland's largest candy factory advertised everywhere as "Cowan's my Sweet" and also helped to sponsor the memorable Billy Graham Crusade at Kelvin Hall in Glasgow. After Aldworth wrote an evangelistic booklet called "My Plan" he asked me to translate it into German for distribution in Europe, a task which gave me great satisfaction. My contact with these men opened many doors for an active evangelistic ministry.

I also visited some of the poorest families who had very little food to eat but nonetheless shared a cup of tea with me. By contrast, I was the key note speaker at an annual youth conference held at the Carnegie Estate in the Midlands. I found myself preaching the Word of God in run-down mission halls and multi-million dollar churches going back to the Middle Ages. Some weekends I travelled with the Scottish Male Voice Festival Choir as they sang in churches and mission halls all over Scotland while I gave my testimony or a short evangelistic message. During college recesses I would find myself climbing the highest mountains in England and Scotland as a tour guide and witnessing Christ to people as they fearfully stared down over a steep cliff. On other occasions I was invited to join an evangelist or inspirational speaker during evangelistic rallies in England, Scotland or Ireland, not to preach but simply to give a short testimony during the service. Much the same happened on the European Continent, especially in Germany and Switzerland, although I was to spend relatively little time in those countries after my conversion.

But the highlight of my evangelistic outreach came with an assignment from the Scottish Evangelistic Council. A young man from Latvia and I signed up for what was known at the time as "colportage work," meaning the house to house sales and distribution of Christian books and Bibles for evangelistic access to families. My co-worker and I were stationed in the village of Gardenstown on the North Eastern Coast of Scotland. We had received permission from the local Church of Scotland minister to park our little camping trailer on his property right behind the manse. Here we had all the warmth and encouragement we needed from the pastor and his devout congregation of about 250 people, most of them fishermen and their families. Riding the rural dirt roads on bicycles with large carriers for our cargo, we visited family homes and farms all over the countryside and sold so many books that our supplier at one point couldn't replenish our supply fast enough! But our mission was not welcomed by everybody. While most of the rural Scottish population is friendly and hospitable toward strangers, there are always some people who feel antagonistic or even hostile toward Christian missionaries. To some degree that was caused by a pseudo Christian cult known as Jehovah's Witnesses. They claimed to base their authority on the Scriptures but had their own interpretation of God's Word, including such deadly errors as rejecting the deity of Christ, His resurrection, and the Trinity. The Witnesses are dedicated zealots and were known for their diligent and sometimes overly persistent visits to private homes. It was especially embarrassing for us that some of them had scoured the countryside prior to our activities, so we devised what we thought was a clever introduction when a resident opened the door: "Hello, we are from the Scottish Evangelistic Council – we are not Jehovah's witnesses." That seemed to work for us quite well for opening new doors until one day, after my "clever" introduction, the lady scrutinizing me responded with a triumphant smile, "but I am!" She invited us into her home anyway, probably thinking that this was her opportunity to win us over to her theology, and graciously offered us a cup of tea during the following very lively discussion. To our surprise the lady bought several of our books and we prayed together before we left. Both of us had learned a profound lesson: Don't allow your preconceptions and prejudice to interfere with any opportunity God gives you to witness to His Word of wisdom and salvation.

It was with a background like this stretching over several years that I received an invitation from the United Free Church of Scotland, as mentioned in the Introduction, to become what they called a "lay missionary" in one of their churches on the Shetland Islands, and my first full-time pastorate. At the time the population on the Island of Unst, the most northerly of the Shetlands, was about 1000 souls, a number that has declined since as most young people were seeking employment on the Scottish mainland. However, it is my understanding that offshore oil drilling has brought many part-time residents along with major technological improvements and a subtle change in culture.

This ecclesiastical appointment was fundamental in shaping my ideas, methods of serving, and interaction with a congregation. With about 125 members it was a small church located on a tiny, remote island about twelve miles long and six miles wide. I had preached in many churches but never been a pastor and soon learned the difference between preaching and teaching, the urgent need for pastoral care, and how a congregation depends on their pastor. The demands on my time and talents were very modest, compared to other churches later. But the desire to build personal relationships was astonishing. It seemed that everybody in the church wanted to be my friend and, no matter what small service I rendered, it was appreciated well beyond my efforts.

I soon discovered that the Shetlanders were a very special group people, and their character had a lot to do with their isolated environment. But their geographical isolation, as I soon discovered, did not mean that they were disconnected from the outside world. The school, which accommodated all grades, offered an excellent education and in some ways these hardy Islanders whose main occupation was crofting (small scale farming) and fishing were as well educated and knowledgeable as people elsewhere – maybe even better. I also discovered that isolation encourages close relationships where everybody knows each other, and, not surprisingly, a striking degree of personal caring. It is well known, of course, that people who work the land and harvest the sea are generally not just physically strong, but morally upright. Add to that a simple but buoyant faith in God, and you have a good picture of the physiognomy of the Shetlanders. There was no crime on the island and no resident sheriff. A police officer from one of the other islands visited the village of Baltasound, where we lived, one day a week, mostly to pick up some fresh herring for which the town was famous.

Apart from preaching on Sundays, congregational visitation was my major activity in during my ministry. There were few cars on the island, so I joined the natives and acquired a little NSU – a one horsepower motor cycle that was assisted by pedals, like a bicycle, which served especially well when going uphill. One of our members lived on the "far" west coast of the island. As a retired university professor who now raised a few cattle and chickens, he had acquired a large library and was amazingly erudite. I enjoyed visiting his croft once a week and we had lively discussions over the steak dinner covering just about every subject known to man. I can honestly say that I learned more from him than he did from me. There were many tears of farewell when, after a little less than a year, I answered God's call to leave the Shetlands and move to Canada.

The Lessons Learned: I did not know it at the time, but God in His providential care was preparing me for missions in very different places, with a wide range of people, and diverse responsibilities. My Shetland experience was formative in shaping my role as a pastor. Even simple but hardy people living without the trappings of modern civilization can exhibit an amazing faith. The servant of God must be prepared to answer His call to serve Him on any place on earth, into any culture, and into what may appear to be at first hopeless opportunities and a waste of time. But always remember this: God never calls a man or woman to serve Him without first equipping them for the task ahead, although at the time they may not know it.

CHAPTER TWO

Understanding the Priority of Your Faith and Mission

The Germans have a definition of the pastor that, in my opinion, comes as close to the purpose of his call as any: "One who cares for the soul." On the surface at least our secularized religion downplays the importance – or even the existence – of the soul, and even many Christians think of the pastor mostly as a "preacher." Add to that the popular notion that he works little more than one hour a week! But the primary concern for the welfare of the soul, as opposed to the body of a person, is surely the most crucial focus of a pastor's work. However, popular unbelief aided by skeptical science and modern life styles have profoundly undermined the idea that man has a soul. Indeed, atheism has for centuries argued the very opposite, namely that men and women are no more than human animals and that all life is terminated when they die.

Those who enter Christian service may not be aware of it at first but they soon learn that for many people, including some of their parishioners, religion is a "cultural cloak" used to make people look more respectable and "all-rounded." Hence, although a young pastor may want to launch out into a hearty ministry of preaching the Word, his first obstacle may be the common existential question, "does God really exist?" To play it safe and to justify their existence many churches advance their social initiatives with the idea of salvation of the soul playing a secondary role. This can be seen in a tolerant and unbiblical "universalism" implying that since "Christ died for all" everybody is saved. The question than remains: Is the most important objective of Christian mission not really directed toward social issues and economic relief? They point to plenty of evidence for this in the Bible, especially in the exhortation of our Lord Jesus to feed the hungry and help the poor, a command further sustained by the teaching of the Apostle James who declares that "faith without works is dead." What some well-meaning Christians miss here is that "faith" comes before "works" like the trunk of a tree grows before its branches. However, the history of Christian missions all over the world with its goal to feed the hungry, heal the sick and "rescue the perishing" clearly demonstrates that true faith must also involve social action as part of our quest for souls in fulfillment of God's commands.

The often used phrase "Minister of the Word and Sacrament" designates the two major functions of the pastor. His preaching duties are usually fulfilled on Sundays at stated times, but they may well extend beyond his congregation. The celebration of the Lord's Supper is held at various times depending on church practice. Presbyterians usually observe a "Communion Service" as it is often called at least once a month. In contrast to the Roman Catholic Church which celebrates the Lord's Supper much more frequently, Protestants generally place less emphasis on it than on the Ministry of Preaching, the importance of which, along with the practice of prayer and teaching, is mentioned several times in the New Testament.

An often cited verse comes from the Book of Romans where the Apostle Paul declares that "faith comes from hearing the message, and the message is heard through the word of Christ," (10:17 NIV). He also urges Timothy to devote himself "to the public reading of Scripture, to preaching and to teaching," (II. Tim. 4:13 NIV). The ability of a minister to "preach the whole counsel of God" is therefore viewed as his most important, though not the only, qualification for the pastorate. It is here, of course, that the priority of a pastor's mission comes into sharpest focus.

Preaching is, like other activities in life, in some ways "an art and a science" as it engages both the mind and the heart of the person with the message. But it is much more than that. The preacher is an instrument in the hands of God and, like a farmer sowing the seed on his soil, his preaching ministry will only be fruitful with God's blessing because only He can make things grow and flourish.

We hear much about the "famous" preachers of our age and their outstanding "charisma" as they proclaim the Word of Salvation. But the Lord can and will also use His Word through lesser lips and much more subdued methods of communication. Jonathan Edwards, the great 19th century revival preacher of New England, is said to have read his sermons with weakened eye sight and a stumbling voice over the flickering light of an oil lamp. Despite this uninspiring style the Spirit of God moved large crowds of people to the conviction of sin and repentance once causing a spiritual revival in his church.

This is not intended to be an essay about the art of homiletics. But because preaching is so important and so many pastors have asked me about my own techniques and experience, I shall note those elements in declaring the Word of Lord that have helped me in my ministry.

First, preaching must be biblical. A Christian man or woman sharing the truth about God has only one authority to rely upon: the Bible, which contains the revealed knowledge of God. Other Christian literature and electronic media may supplement His abiding truth, but the Christian faith is solely based on God's Word: ***sole scriptura,*** as Martin Luther would say.

Second, preaching must be rational. God gave us His Word not to confuse us but to enlighten and teach us. His truth is not speculation but revelation; the characters and events of Scripture and not fictional, but historical; the Bible is not hypothetical but practical. Beyond its amazing scholarship, God intends that His Word is accessible and plausible to all men.

Third, preaching must be factual. It is important to declare the whole counsel of God by staying with recorded events and experiences as they are told by the Biblical writers. Personal interpretations can be novel and informative, but they should never override the central truth that is taught.

The inspired Canon of Scripture (approved by the Church Fathers) allows no omissions, insertions, or revisions.

Fourth, preaching must be practical. By that I mean that messages from the pulpit should be simple in language, eloquent in style, and convincing in logic. Apart from its eternal truth shining through the ages and overwhelming all theories and philosophies, it must also be relevant to the needs of the audience. The core beliefs of Scripture never change, but how they are applied to different cultures may.

Finally, peaching should be memorable. A person can only remember what he or she hears and understands in the first place. Every preacher should know that people's attention span is no more than 20 minutes – if they are attentive at all. Hour-long sermons may drone on and on but their effectiveness is questionable, no matter how eloquently presented. One often hears remarks about "truly spirit-filled sermons" and that is good, but God knows our limitations and in my experience such messages are relatively short and to the point. Sometimes humorous situations arise like the one I will share here. Half a dozen young men, all formally dressed in suits and ties, were sitting on the stage of an auditorium facing a large audience in Glasgow, Scotland. They were all graduates from a well-known Bible and missionary training college and had been charged to summarize their college experiences in a short address exceeding no more than 5 minutes, giving the group half an hour or so in the ceremony. Alas, finally the last student, a young man from London, stood up to speak to a restless audience that had listened to personal anecdotes for well over 45 minutes and expecting more to come. He gave the most popular speech of all: "Ladies and gentlemen, my address today is "1403 Plymouth Avenue, London, England. Thank you!" A roaring crowd gave him a standing ovation and I learned a sobering lesson: With some qualifications, the shortest speeches are the most popular!

There is one innovative technique for preaching sermons I learned and found useful as a student pastor and carried over into my future pulpit preaching. It also works for professional and business speeches, and even some lectures when appropriate. It is called "alliteration" which matches

Biblical phrases with similar sounding words that make following a sermon easier. An example comes from Paul's description of the gospel in Romans 1:16 which could be alliterated with three points as "the Existence of a Danger, the Experience of a Dynamic, and the "Emphasis on a Decision."

The first lesson I learned in my early ministry beginning on the Island of Unst in the Shetlands was that I'd better be prepared to give an account of my faith – not only ***what*** I believed but ***why*** I believed what I believed. I soon discovered a need to incorporate "apologetics" (the defense of the faith") in my sermons because some of the members of the church typically considered the Christian ministry more of a social than a spiritual effort. Just as I discovered in some other churches, there existed some confusion in the sense that some well-meaning folk tended to assign greater priority to social relief than to winning souls. It is important to understand that such a subtle unbelief can be as much of a problem in the church as outside the church. While many of the hardy Islanders in my congregation had a Biblical faith in God, some of them clearly considered the institution of the church as mostly a cultural or communal necessity.

"Inspired ignorance" is one of the worst enemies in the church and often expressed in the most ludicrous ways. I knew a man in Canada whose stunning naivety made him confidently declare that as an "educated man" he could never believe in God because "he could not believe in anything that he could see" and it was "logical" that things unseen could not possibly exist. There are, of course, many people like him who never made a commitment to Christ, reminding us of the apostle's teaching that we are "dead in transgressions and sins" (Eph. 2:1 NIV) with the logical implication that dead men cannot see – or understand. But the problem of ignorance is much more subtle than that. Even believers who are quite familiar with the Scriptures, including pastors, can display an appalling ignorance about the key doctrines of Scripture including the central truth of Christ's vicarious death on the Cross, His resurrection, and His promised return. One reason for the decline of the major religious denominations in the United States is the rejection of Biblical authority in many areas of life, something that happened also in Germany and helped the rise of totalitarian movements caused by a widespread rejection of the moral standards taught in the Bible. It is also a reminder that the gift of faith and the endowment of the Holy Spirit are required to open our eyes to the full truth of God's counsel.

The priority of the Church's mission is to announce to the world the Gospel or "Good News" that Christ died for our sins and that all those who believe in Him will have their souls saved for eternity. Whatever else follows is secondary – important, compassionate, caring – but secondary. Those who make it the first priority of the church may be "inspired to do good" but I call it "inspired ignorance." The teaching and preaching of the Gospel for man's eternal salvation is clearly a greater and more enduring benefit than even the most ambitious and effective social action a church can be involved in and clearly supersedes even the most urgently needed efforts to relieve physical suffering. However, it is noteworthy that, for example, the great English mission societies started in the 19th century never neglected to minister to the bodily needs of their native populations and one missionary once told me: "You can't preach to people with empty stomachs."

There is no doubt that a Christian witness based on God's revelation must take into account the whole person and I have never met a Christian worker or pastor who would question that. The argument is one of priority, not a choice of one over the other and that is shown vividly by the Salvation Army ministries where hungry people are given a meal before they hear the gospel.

While living in Mexico I agreed to serve a non-denominational church in response to the leadership's request of simply "preaching the Word." The congregation consisted mostly of expatriates from the United States and Canada and it represented just about every denomination. However, as is the case with many non-denominational churches, because of their all-inclusiveness they tend to be less specific in matters of doctrine than we may find in the historic denominations. With the enthusiastic cooperation of most of the elders we quickly drew up a statement of faith and changed the focus of their mission to the teaching and preaching of God's word in the church while also maintaining a social ministry to students and other needy individuals in the community. Not everybody understood the changes and I noticed a bit of "inspired ignorance" but most of the congregation accepted my leadership and the response to our worship services and other activities was gratifying. I also realized, with the help of others, that the main reason for what some people in the congregation perceived as an over-emphasis on social outreach was mostly due to ignorance of what the Bible is teaching – a not uncommon situation suggesting that the basic gospel message was not very well understood.

Because my wife, daughter and I had plans to move to South America I had committed myself to serving the church for not more than one year. In order to make the message of the saving life of Christ as effective as possible - with the church leadership's support - I began my ministry with preaching the basic Biblical truths combined with "the defense of the faith." These lectures are designed to address the common skepticism people have about God, Christ and eternity. As I had done elsewhere, lectures about such subjects as "Is the Bible Really the Word of God?", "Does Modern Science Support the Historical Record of the Bible?" and "Was Jesus Really Who He said He was?" proved to be effective teaching tools and helped some people to understand metaphysical realities. More importantly, it also brought conviction of sin and the need for personal salvation to some in the church and even in the community. While representing a not uncommon phenomenon of a church without a clearly defined Christian theology and mission, I became acquainted with similar manifestations of theological ignorance and a misunderstanding of priorities in other pastorates.

The Lessons Learned: There is no substitute for faithfully "declaring the whole counsel of God" for edification and sanctification and also for winning souls, although the pastor's responsibility may not be primarily evangelism. Ignorance of Christ and His atoning work among church members is one of the **most** discouraging phenomena a pastor can face, and one of the most urgent reasons for a Christ-centered ministry. It can be combatted on historical and theological grounds but conquering a man's mind and heart with the knowledge of Christ is largely a work of the Holy Spirit. But I also learned never to underestimate the spiritual wisdom of church members who, despite the discouragement of secularism in the place of worship, expressed an amazing awareness of the power of Christ and the potential for positive change. I expected and sometimes met with opposition and disapproval, but one must never waiver in one's faith but stand steadfast in the mission of proclaiming Christ against all odds.

CHAPTER THREE

Keeping the Gospel Pure

From its earliest beginnings the Church had to learn to protect the purity of its teaching with vigilance and tenacity. We see this in almost all of the Epistles, and the Apostle Paul's warnings were no idle talk. It seems that satanic forces are always at work to confuse, distort, pervert and cause doubt about the meaning of God's Word. Without much caution and circumspection, most churches eventually face the danger of diluting and compromising God's marvelous truth, and usually for no other obvious reason than a lack of faith in God's revealed Word and its profound meaning for the salvation of the soul.

I have seen and heard of examples of this throughout my pastoral ministry. But some experiences stand out as unusually radical manifestation of attempts, albeit usually out of ignorance rather than malice, to distort the truth of the Gospel. As anyone who has ever served a church knows, doctrinal extremes can cause conflict and divisions. For example, I have never ceased to be amazed how such ideas as "moral perfection," "salvation through works" or a smug sense of self-righteousness can be nurtured in so many churches and so deeply affect the total and comprehensive efficacy of Christ's atonement on the Cross.

During the course of my ministry I encountered more than one example of a church which confused the priority of its mission in that it clearly favored social action over the Biblical message of personal salvation. In some of my own pastorates, but also in the many churches I visited as guest speaker, I learned of problems which deeply affected the spiritual health and unity of God's people while also sensing an eagerness to learn more about the Lord Jesus Christ and the meaning of the priorities set by a living faith in Christ. I hope that I am not overly judgmental when, for the sake of alerting young pastors and Christian workers to what they can expect in their service for the Lord, I am offering some examples in this book. I might add that many other pastors have shared similar experiences and stories indicating that these problems are not uncommon but helped to reinforce my conviction that there is always a need for vigilance to "keep the gospel pure."

Because the problems of the church tend to be universal, I shall give a few examples of the issues and concerns that are common in the pastorate without implicating any particular congregation or individual. After all, God is the only Judge of how we define, arrange, and execute our ecclesiastical affairs, but we can learn what is best by applying Biblical principles and teaching to these issues and hopefully learn from the mistakes of others as we also learn from our own.

My own ministry, extending over half a century, taught me many lessons from my own activities in the pastorate and from others. I observed - and sometimes became involved in - a number of issues and events that illuminate the ecclesiastical landscape in a somewhat negative way, but never without also shedding the light of hope and peace that comes from the Cross. As pointed out above, more often than not I saw that diverse viewpoints of doctrine could lead to endless controversy and extremes in church policy. I shall confine my observations to a few areas that were the most prominent in my experience, but I am sure that others pastors can add similar stories from their own ministry and many more.

"Keeping the gospel pure" essentially means that we declare the "whole counsel of God" within a Biblical consensus and without apology, although even within that consensus there will be different views in the vast details of theological argument and Biblical interpretation. However, the central and vital truth of the Gospel is not difficult to understand. It is that Jesus died on the cross for sinners and calls us to Him for repentance, faith and commitment so that we may receive the gift of eternal life. Any teaching in the church which does not focus on that priority may be commendable and comforting – but it is not the Gospel. Beyond that we must insist that the Scriptures are expounded truthfully with a clear eye on what God is teaching us. God's revelation in the Bible is not subject to speculation and fantasy. Facts, not fiction is what the Lord wants us to hear, yet throughout history the church has battled through waves of heresy and deliberately falsified accounts of historical events and theological doctrines. Even a very basic study of church history shows the endless battles that have been fought for the authenticity and accuracy of Biblical teaching and the fight for the preservation of the ultimate truth about God and man. There are, of course, even today detractors and detractions, and in various shapes and forms distortions and even perversions of the gospel are commonly found throughout Christendom.

Beyond the danger of preaching and teaching that we might simply call as "unbiblical" because it violates its historical or theological veracity, the purity of the gospel can also be endangered by unchristian attitudes and actions. The false perceptions created by any conduct claimed to be Christian when it is not can seriously damage our witness to Christ. Unfortunately, it happens all the time.

Before we delve further into this important area of what sometimes can be honest mistakes mixed with willful error, a lack of dedicated Bible teaching, and a genuine desire to serve God in a capacity other than presenting the central theme of the Gospel, let me point out that in cases where I could be a mediator or where my advice was welcome, my objective was always the same: Maintain the peace and unity of the church and let the glorious gospel triumph over all divisions while healing the "Body of Christ" for His glory.

The first example of what the gospel is not concerns the phenomenon of spiritual pride illustrated with an incident of a woman who owned and operated a liquor store. Well known in the little town where she lived and worked she was generally respected and viewed as a good citizen. However, in at least one of the churches there was an overriding sentiment that a Christian woman could not possibly be engaged in such a business. Without tapping into the depth of moral theology which rules, and not without good reasons, that alcohol and the Christian faith do not mix well, many Christians would consider such a position as legalistic. While they may admit that the Bible warns against drunkenness, there is no clear prohibition against all alcoholic beverages. This is demonstrated by the different social mores governing alcohol in various countries and cultures and the variety of views taken by Christians regarding the matter.

In any case, after a new pastor in the community visited with the liquor store owner and successfully corrected her opinion that all Christians were self-righteous, she started going to church and eventually made a decision for Christ. The question remains: How many people like this woman feel excluded from the church and the gospel because they have met Christians with narrowly defined legalistic views that have the result of discouraging them from ever entering the door of a church?

It may seem strange but evangelical zeal, while presenting the gospel, can also go to the peculiar extreme which I shall call here "the quest for moral perfection." There is, of course, nothing wrong with any Christian who earnestly strives to live his life more and more according to the high moral standards set before us in God's Word. But it is not the process of "growing in grace" or what we also call "sanctification" I am talking about. Rather, we are confronting the disturbing phenomenon of some very serious moralists who have espoused the belief that, with the help of the Holy Spirit, a person can become morally perfect on this side of eternity – or nearly so. Striving for such a condition may not sound so bad and even commendable. But apart from the obvious error that the objective of moral perfection can never be obtained while we live in the flesh, there is a grave danger here in that moral self-effort can cloud and diminish the death of Christ on the Cross, thus making His vicarious atonement no longer efficacious.

I have seen this reach for perfect morals in several places but in one case it gravely impeded the vital ministry of one church that used to be a powerhouse for the gospel. Although only a few of its members were involved in the cult of moral perfectionism, the negative impact on the purity of the gospel was profound and many people left the church because of it.

There is unfortunately nothing new about this false craving for impeccable morals which has been a problem for the church throughout the centuries, but God does not expect His servants to be paragons of moral virtue. Nonetheless, as far back as in the Middle Ages we had a fanatic, self-destructive group of religious zealots known as the "Flagellants" who were convinced that they needed to punish their bodies as part of truly effective repentance. They walked through the streets of medieval towns beating each other bloody with chains and other objects, implying that the death of our Savior on the Cross was not enough to make atonement for our sins.

There have always been moral perfectionists and I had various encounters with some of them during my ministry. But the notion flies in the face of Scripture which clearly teaches that the Lord Jesus gave His life for our sins "once and for all." This all-sufficiency of His sacrifice is hammered home by the Apostle Paul in many of his epistles such as his letter to the Romans where he writes about God's righteousness coming "through faith in Jesus Christ to all who believe," (Rom. 3:22 NIV). This verse was to be one of the cornerstones of the Protestant Reformation and Luther's key-doctrine for defying the Papal decrees advocating a need for "good works" to "supplement and ensure" the complete efficacy of Christ's death of the Cross.

It is truly amazing that there are still today so-called Christians who reject Christ's atonement with a false belief that human self-effort can somehow add to the merits of their personal salvation. "You cannot plate gold," somebody has said, which is a good example that we can do nothing to "improve" His atoning sacrifice. The inevitable results of such an erroneous belief are feelings of worthlessness, fruitless pursuits of self-denial, and a highly legalistic attitude toward Christians who believe that their salvation is "through Christ alone."

A lack of understanding the Bible is, of course, a problem in many churches and sometimes based on personal prejudice. While this is mostly due to a lack of authentic Bible teaching, sometimes the reasons are more obscure and even somewhat amusing. This was expressed by one indignant lady who stood up during an adult Sunday School class and declared that in her opinion the Apostle Paul had "one shipwreck too many." She was referring to several of his moral exhortations which she deemed unrealistic. Unfortunately we are not free to pick and choose statements and passages from the Bible according to our own preferences and preconceived notions about what is true and what is not.

The Lessons Learned: Keeping the gospel pure is not an easy task. A diligent study of Biblical truth and understanding clearly what God is teaching us and the careful preservation of all Holy Writ is of primary importance to the church. We must guard against pride, the greatest of all sins and unforgivable if it prevents us from seeking God. Self-righteousness and ideas about self-induced moral perfection have no place in the "Good News" about the soul's salvation and any preconceived notions defining right and wrong outside of God's grace have no permanent effect on our destiny. There can never be any compromise about these core teachings of God's Word. Some aspects of this subject are further dealt with later in this book.

CHAPTER FOUR

Making the Gospel Relevant to Our Age

When reminding people that Biblical revelation must always be seen in its historical context there are those who may suspect that I am trying to diminish in some way its potent message for all ages. What I am trying to do as an evangelical Christian is really to make the eternal Word of God relevant to our times, even to give certain national celebrations like Memorial Day or Independence Day a hi-lighted illumination in the light of God's Word.

When applying Biblical wisdom to contemporary issues and events, the pastoral message must always reflect the realities of good and evil in the world. The well-known song "This is my Father's world," while having some truth in it, can mislead us into thinking that we live in an ideal instead of in a fallen world over which God our Creator has given temporary authority to Satan, the master strategist of all evil. We see Satan at work throughout history and so often evil triumphing over good, both in individuals, communities and nations. I have seen pastors get so entangled in the stories of the Old Testament, for example, that their conclusions are closer to history lessons than the explanation of the profound spiritual truths God is teaching us in the world we live today. But then there are also those who want to apply every detail of the Old Testament record written millennia ago to current events. That may apply to prophecies, of course, as well as other events about our long salvation history, but there are divine truths, like those of atonement sacrifices, that were specifically about ancient customs peculiar to that era. To make and keep God's Word alive and arousing we must show the impact of its truth on the lives of people today who are trying to make a living from eight to five, raising a family on limited resources, feeling economically insecure, perhaps discriminated against or even socially ostracized and facing an uncertain future. The phrase "pie in the sky" was coined in response to preaching, no matter how sincere, that seemed to overlook the daily needs of working people who had little time or interest for refinements of profound theological discussions that had no plausible or practical application to their daily lives.

One area of potential conflict in the United States lies in the often mentioned tense relationship between church and state, a widely misunderstood issue. The law intends to keep church and state apart so that the church, on one hand, can never usurp political power and the state, on the other, cannot interfere with the religious freedom and mission of the church. While it is true that in practice this law is not always easily defined in favor of one or the other, the separation of church and state is designed to benefit both by preventing a theocracy of the type we see in Islamic countries where governments in most cases use strongly tendentious religious doctrines to override civil liberties, effectively punishing unbelievers and those of other faiths.

The separation of church and state does not mean that men and women of God held to the highest standards of morality and public policy have to be silent in light of political overreach and government excesses. While political opinion is essentially a private matter reflecting personal preferences, being a Christian, and especially a Church leader, does not mean that one has to be non-political or a duty to "ride the fence on both sides." There is a clear call to what the Biblical writers call "righteousness," a rich word which includes such concepts as justice, the dignity of man, human equality, personal freedom, moral uprightness, and many more. To the extent that unjust and unrighteous politics affect the welfare of every citizen, the church must speak out in protest when a government promulgates laws and engages in actions that are, in its opinion, contrary to national interest or even a clear violation of basic human rights. The moral standards set forth in the statutes of God's righteous laws as proclaimed in the Book of Proverbs state with one word what our Creator expects from us morally: "Righteousness exalts a nation, but sin is a disgrace to any people" (14:34 NIV). The Biblical writer was pointing out the punishment for nations that defied God many centuries ago, and that is still happening in the world today. It is a lesson that should not be lost on those countries today that have learned nothing from history and are steering their ship of state into a deadly storm of divine retribution.

The Bible offers a grim lesson for individuals and nations alike as the ancient prophets warned the rulers and their people of God's coming judgments. Their tragic fulfillment makes up much of Old Testament history, but the story does not end there. Throughout history we read about rulers and nations who were "good" or "evil," and in modern times nobody has forgotten just how evil a government can be when it turns its back on God and His moral standard demanding "righteousness." Modern nations like Germany, to name one, a country favored and blessed by God with the Protestant Reformation in the 16th century that changed the world, less than a century later started denying the authenticity of many Scriptural passages thereby undermining their moral authority. But by repudiating the trustworthiness of the Scriptures, and even declaring the need to "demythologize" many of the Bible stories recorded for us, they caused the creeping moral and spiritual decay of many churches. Millions of people now rejected the Gospel of Christ. God's judgment fell on the nation as people were blinded by their choice of political and moral leadership with the worst destructive satanic forces coming to power. They were to quickly destroy the former land of Martin Luther and erode the spectacular benefits of the Protestant Reformation during World War II.

Even in countries where there is no *de jure* separation of church and state as in Germany where the official Lutheran Church, unlike many other denomination, is considered part of the state (known as the principle of "Erastianism") pastors have no problem exercising their right to criticize the government and denounce political doctrines and actions contrary to Christian belief. A clear example is the opposition of the Confessing Church (the evangelical segment of the Lutheran Church during and after the Second World War) to the Nazi State. When the Church is no longer the conscience of the State all restraints on absolute power are abolished and tyranny lurks right around the corner.

Having said that, a Christian's involvement in political and other civic issues is limited and overshadowed by God's call to love and serve all people. Partisan politics offer a dangerous opportunity for bias and distortion of the truth as one can plausibly argue that no one party is never completely right or wrong about everything all the time. Confronting controversial social and political issues is always a delicate task for the pastor, especially when preaching from the pulpit. My own efforts have been to identify the most important issues, view them in the context of Scripture whenever relevant, and then denouncing what is wrong by taking a stand for what is right, carefully avoiding political arguments which often generate more heat than light. The congregation usually knows what I am talking about without going into partisan politics. Above all my witness to Christ's love and the need for men and women to repent of sin and turn to Him for their salvation must never be sidelined in favor of any political argument, no matter how important it appears to be. In the final analysis we can safely reaffirm the sovereignty of God, knowing that everything on earth, including political corruption and injustice, are under His complete control. There is no clearer evidence for this than in the great historical events called national revivals.

To mention just one, John Wesley, along with his brother Charles, were servants of God called to be agents of a mighty national reformation by means of a spiritual revival. In the eighteenth century England had degenerated into what seemed a hopeless degree of moral and ethical decay, along with widespread political corruption and a near breakdown of the justice system. Within less than a decade Wesley's preaching with a call to repentance and faith in Christ literally changed the nation, resulting not only in the birth of the Methodist Church, but in widespread and lasting social reforms in such areas as the penal system, alcoholism and prostitution. It led eventually even to the abolition of slavery in the British

Empire. Unfortunately, Wesley in later years drifted into the non-Biblical doctrine of "near moral perfection" which became part of the Arminianism of the Methodist or Wesleyan Church. Its core teaching was that man had a "free will" to choose God, a notion that was rejected by Calvin whose theological centerpiece was the sovereignty of God which could never be overruled by any man. These distinctively different theological doctrines are in opposition to each other to this day.

One has to remember that unless God revives us from within, there is little chance of national reform and renewal on the outside. One of the greatest lessons taught by history is that spiritual revival must precede political and social reform in order to produce real change. It is often said that our nation "needs God more than ever today," but the truth is that a nation needs God all the time because without Him a nation cannot be righteous and prosper. The Old Testament contains a disturbing record of what happens to nations when they disobey God. Their doom is sealed unless they repent, and severe retribution is reserved for those who disobey.

But whether in politics, the economy, the justice system, sports, entertainment or popularized religion, the people in the pew need the assurance that God is just as real today as He was in the ancient days of Moses and Jeremiah, and that He speaks to us in every age with clarity and relevance to our needs. It is not always an easy task to preach the gospel with a sense of immediate urgency in the context of contemporary events, but without it people tend to get bored and indifferent to what we preach. Finally, it is Erwin Lutzer who summarizes this matter most eloquently: "We must not be intimidated by those who wish to silence the mouths of ministers under the guise of the separation of church and state. But we must also remember that our message is not a political agenda but the full biblical mandate of submission to the will of God." See "Pastor to Pastor," p.52, Kregel Publications, 1998.

There is yet another area of concern about making our Biblical messages relevant to our times. This relates to a pastor's theology and the emphasis he may give it from his theological studies or other influences. There are of course a considerable number of theological interpretations of the

Bible, as the history of various denominations (Lutheran, Methodist, Congregational, Baptist, Presbyterian, Pentecostal, etc.) clearly shows. For many years well-meaning Christians expressed their theological preference, which was usually also exhibited in the form of their worship service, by joining a denomination in which they grew up, became acquainted with through marriage, or, perhaps most importantly, chose because they found Christ in that church.

There is, of course, nothing wrong with adhering to a particular set of doctrines based on the Scriptures. The problem arises when a person begins to think that his or her theological preference is superior to all others because it more accurately reflects a particular doctrine of Biblical teaching. Even that posture may have a place as long as it does not downgrade or even ridicule other theological preferences. But what might be called "denominationalism" can lead to a false pride and a narrow legalism that consistently dwells on a particular subject, often man's unworthiness. This is deadly for a pastor who wants to reach out to everybody in his church, including those people of faith who have never been interested in the fine points and differences of our great theological heritage. To illustrate this point I suggest that few evangelical Christians today are knowledgeable or even care much about the differences in the theology of Martin Luther, who put sinful man and his need for justification into the center of his doctrines, or John Calvin whose emphasis was on the grace and sovereignty of God. But nobody would argue that they were wrong. In fact, both were right and nobody could claim to be a "better" Christian on account of preferring one theology over the other.

I already mentioned our need to be relevant in the pulpit for political and socio-economic reasons, but our "theology" must be equally relevant if we are to teach and reach our congregations in today's society. Dogma, defined by Webster as "a body of doctrines concerning faith and morals formally stated and authoritatively proclaimed by a church" is much less a part of people's immediate religious concerns than it used to be. The slow faltering of our great historical denominations in many parts of the country and the rise of "interdenominational" and "non-denominational" churches teaches us a simple lesson: Christians are more interested in the direct teaching of the Bible than in the formulations of different theologies that are derived from it. Whatever is the explanation of this trend, the fact is that the major difference for Christians in America today is whether one is an "evangelical" (Bible-believing) or a "nominal" (socially focused) Christian. It is a fact that many of our churches today have members worshiping together in one church who come from various theological backgrounds.

All of this poses a real challenge for a pastor, but it does not have to be a problem. The Word of God in its marvelous revelation is rich enough for anyone to tap into and mine the truths necessary to proclaim the essentials of the Christian faith. This does not require a formal historic doctrine of theology, desirable as it may be for a greater in-depth understanding of our theological heritage. Moreover, for local churches this trend away from dogma does not negate the need for a clear statement of faith that is commonly held by all evangelical Christians.

There is no better place to investigate the failure of denominationalism than looking at an example of a church that failed and fell because of it, although, as is common in these situations, there were also other factors that led to its decline. After my retirement in Florida, I became acquainted with a small but very active denominational church with a very dedicated and committed pastor that started to develop problems with attendance and finances. Intelligent, well informed, and an excellent expositor of Scripture in the pulpit the pastor was known and respected as an excellent preacher. However, I heard complaints that his constant emphasis on denominational doctrines emphasizing man's unworthiness, without balancing his message with God's overriding grace, had resulted in negative reactions by many of the worshipers. They apparently started to feel like a patient who is told again and again by his physician that he is very ill without learning about a cure. Here are my own thoughts about such a situation.

When preaching about sin and eternal punishment it is important to remember the Apostle Paul's teaching about law and grace, summarized by the fundamental truth that "where sin abounded, grace did much more abound," (Rom. 5:20 AV).The majority of worshipers did not need constant reminders that they were sinners – they needed the encouragement of the cure. Sadly, despite this pastor's excellent sermons, his dedication to Christ, and his genuine efforts to be a leader of his people, his outstanding pulpit ministry eventually lost the support of a sizeable part of the congregation which decided to leave the church. After his resignation attendance eventually dwindled to a few eventually causing the suspension of church services. The young minister left the community for another pastorate and one can only hope and pray that his great gifts of teaching and preaching will be greatly used by the Lord in other places.

However, in fairness to the pastor it must also be understood that a declining church is never all his fault. A keener awareness of the problem and identifying its causes earlier perhaps combined with a greater urgency in helping correct the problem by the leadership and members of the congregation might have avoided a disaster. Perhaps even intervention from fellow pastors in his denomination might have been helpful and avoided the collapse of a vital Christian witness in that community.

This is a sad story indeed, but it illustrates the need for "Biblical relevance" in the pulpit. In Florida, a prime retirement state, the church population is as diverse as in any state I have ministered. Worshipers come from a variety of denominations and in the church that is the subject of this discussion I heard that the people came from many different areas of the country – and, more importantly, from just about every doctrinal preference. Predictably, such a congregation does not find a strong emphasis on a particular church dogma appealing, no matter how important it is historically, in support of Biblical wisdom, and the preferential focus of the pastor's personal beliefs. Finally, this does not dispose of the need for a theological education to include teaching the cardinal doctrines of the Scriptures and the historic Confessions of the church regardless of the denomination. They are a necessity for the lectern, but not always appropriate in the pulpit.

The Lessons Learned: Our witness for Christ and call to repentance of sin does not exempt us from political activism demanding the pursuit of righteousness, justice and peace from our leaders. Politics may be just an example, but the pastor should be involved in all other public affairs and events. There are few areas of life that are that are not exempt from moral scrutiny as they affect the lives of millions of people whose dignity and freedom are affected by national and international events. It is absurd to accept any rule of government that forces pastors to be silent in order for churches to have tax exempt status. Their conscience to speak out against any actions of government or other organizations that violate the Constitution or the Bill of Rights must never be muzzled by arrogant politicians, government and business leaders, or anyone else who think they stand next to God. History demonstrates that disaster follows when the voices of justice and humanity are silenced in the face of political, economic, and social abuses.

But relevance is also very important for a pastor's teaching and preaching, no matter how eloquent he may be. A more inclusive doctrinal approach to Biblical preaching that places less emphasis on denominational theology and relates Biblical truth more appropriately to the culture of our day, perhaps combined with greater personal outreach and a focus on pastoral care, are vital to a minister's effectiveness as a spiritual leader and to the healthy growth of a church.

CHAPTER FIVE

Getting Involved in the Community

It is the pastor's primary responsibility to minister to the congregation, but becoming involved in community affairs and activities should never be far behind. Most congregations would agree that the church is not a private religious retreat for the "elect," but must convey its message beyond the walls of the sanctuary. As one might expect, some pastors are very good at this, while others prefer to seek refuge in their studies.

Unfortunately, equal opportunity for community involvement does not exist. Each town or village is unique, and pastors are not always welcome to participate in some community activities, while in others there simply are not many opportunities for the pastor to play an effective role. But there was no lack of opportunity for work and witness in my following church assignment.

In Lamar, Colorado, a town near the border of Kansas, I served a congregation of about 200 members, and a small satellite church in Bristol, about twenty miles distant. The first chance for community involvement came when the director of continuing education at the Lamar Community College asked me to consider teaching courses as diverse as European history and stress psychology. Next, a police officer in our church asked me to teach a course in stress psychology to the police department, after that to the city personnel staff and then to other groups. Later a nurse in the congregation approached me with a proposal to help start a hospice for the terminally ill. After we also enrolled a physician in that project it became a reality and eventually very successful.

But the greatest challenge for community involvement came when the Neoplan Corporation of Germany, one of the world's biggest manufacturers of buses, bought a large parcel of land outside the town and built a manufacturing plant on it. After meeting a couple of times with their CEO he asked me to join their board as a consultant on labor and management relations. This position was quite formidable because the company faced opposition from no less than three labor unions, all clamoring for higher wages and benefits than the company had planned to pay. Rural Colorado is not Detroit and wages here, even in industrial production, were about half of those in that once famous car manufacturing center.

Gottlieb Auwaerter, the German owner and president of the company, at a special dinner in Lamar, informed me that the company had moved to Lamar not only because of readily available "inexpensive" labor, but also to help with the high seasonal unemployment rate. The company soon faced three labor unions strongly opposed to the compensation rates even though, at my suggestion, the workers received new fringe benefits including profit sharing. But the fight with the unions began nonetheless. Numerous meetings were held, some in the dead of night, as the unions tried to organize the workers, and the company tried hard to keep their employees union-free. At the end the company won by a narrow vote in their favor, and I was given some of the credit for helping resolve the complicated issues for the benefit of the company and ultimately the workers. But credit must also be given to other men and women who worked diligently to shut the unions out and make this a "free labor" project. Had the unions prevailed, Gottlieb Auswaerter had assured me, the new plant would have been nothing more than a "parts warehouse."

The result of all these "extracurricular" activities was not only a big surge in the economy of the whole region, but the church grew also, along with new opportunities for witnessing to various sectors of the community. As mentioned above, I was invited to teach courses as part of the continuing education programs for adults at Lamar Community College but also became involved in some personnel management affairs at NEOPLAN.

Another example of community involvement is provident by my ministry at the Pioneer United Church in Del Norte. Because I served that congregation longer than any other church in my ministry, my time in the San Luis Valley offers a variety of memorable activities and experiences some of which I shall draw upon later in this book. In any case, for the purpose of this chapter I can simply record the fact that I did become very involved in the community when, in addition to being a pastor of a growing congregation, I also taught high school as a substitute teacher and found that after I was elected president of the Parent-Teacher Association I made many new friends and was able to expand my influence as a minister of the gospel.

But beyond being involved in community affairs, the pastor should also make an effort to make friends with his flock. The extent of this much depends on how deeply he wishes to become involved in the personal lives of people, and also on the length of his service to a congregation. During my five-year ministry in Del Norte I made more friends in that church than in any other. Christian friendship is not only mentioned but encouraged in the Bible, and often emulated by our knowledge that Jesus is known as a "friend of sinners." In one famous passage our Lord declares that "greater love has no one than this, that he lay down his life for his friends," (John 15:13 NIV) and during the same encounter he says to his disciples "I no longer call you servants, because a servant does not know his master's business. Instead, I have called you friends for everything I have learned from my Father I have made known to you," (v.15 NIV). This is very significant as social and spiritual intimacy comes from gaining more and more knowledge about a person. It is not difficult to relate this to pastoral friendships – the more a spiritual leader gets to know a person, the more effective he will be in understanding and ministering to his or her needs.

As in all personal relationships, "overreach" can give the appearance of favoritism, and that can be a problem as we are prone by nature to like some people more than others. It is a perception the pastor needs to avoid, but it does not have to become a problem if he opens the door to be a friend to anyone in the church. Most people will understand that some connect better with certain people than with others, but that making individual friendships in the church and in the community is important for the spiritual impact on both, as well as the growth of the congregation.

In the friendly, warm hearted and outgoing congregation of Del Norte making friends was easy and rewarding. It was important for me to study and understand the life and habits of the community. This small town in a big valley was surrounded by snow-capped mountains most of the year. A famous ski area was only miles away, and skiing was a popular sport. So, I learned to ski and made friends in the process. The fall hunting season was a ritual as old as the community itself. So I went hunting with men from the church and some solid friendships developed over time. By the way, I learned quickly that my hunting skills were limited. I never shot an elk or a deer during several seasons of trudging the high mountains in search of prey!

But then there was something else. The lure of not just enjoying the spectacular mountain scenery from the road, or even from fairly accessible mountain parks accessible by car on forest service access, but by using the old mining trails of the past, many of them leading all the way up to mountain passes and peaks measuring over 13,000 ft. There were essentially only two modes of transportation one could use to ascend to such lofty heights: A capable horse or a "dirt bike" (motor cycle) adapted and tuned for high altitudes. It requires a determined and self-confident man or woman to use a motor cycle and drive up a steep, narrow trail strewn with loose rocks and breathing the air that gets more rarified with every 100 ft. climb. Some trails are for experts only – so dangerous that only a man's quick reactions drawn from years of experience can insure survival.

Over time, some men from the congregation and others from the community joined our little group, moving dirt bikes on pick-up trucks (the motorcycles are not licensed for riding on public highways) to more and more remote areas and seeking out ever more "challenging" mountain trails. Eventually the group became known as "Heller's Angels" but as our ambitions grew into ever greater challenges it eventually shrank in size from over two dozen to about seven enthusiasts. My oldest son, a motor cycle endurance racing champion many times over, was an integral part of the gang and a master of evaluating the degree of difficulty of a particular trail that looked as interesting to him as it was scary for me. He often helped me negotiate my machine over territory so steep and hostile that most people would have refused to hike there, let alone ride a motorcycle. We became a closely knit group of professional men, ranchers and businessmen enjoying a unique camaraderie and our reputation became known far beyond the San Luis Valley. A few of us are close friends to this day, decades later, and only the Lord knows how enriched our community was because of these activities. Who can measure the emotional and spiritual impact such men made on each other as they enjoyed such an unusual sport in the high mountains of Colorado? I have never known a group of men so decent and dedicated to the more noble things in life, albeit not every one of them attended my church.

And then there was mountain climbing. This is a sport that requires some planning and more time than I had usually available. Again, in the company of church members and other people from the community we climbed such "fourteeners" (mountains over 14,000 feet) as Uncompagre in the San Juan Mountains and Blanca Peak in the Sangre de Cristo range. This activity we also enjoyed in Estes Park where I served the congregation of the First Baptist Church on "special assignment" as I shall mention later. Here one of our targets was the famous Longs Peak (14,110 ft.) which I climbed with two deacons from the church, one being a mountain guide over the age of 70 who had climbed the peak some fourteen times previously. Perhaps it is the rarified air, but I always had the impression that talking about our faith and praying at 14,000 ft. gave us a special sense of exhilaration!

But the special activities that seemed to top them all were trips to Europe. I had travelled to Europe with my students during college recesses, but those were known as "interterm" study trips designed to broaden the knowledge of students who could afford them. The trips with church and community members were vacations with the purpose of broadening their understanding of Christian cultures in foreign countries. Most of our tour participants had never been out of the country and some never traveled beyond the borders of Colorado. One couple, both eighty years of age and old time ranchers in the San Luis Valley described one of our trips as "the adventure of a lifetime." They had rarely been out of the valley and only a few times out of the state during their retirement years.

Using some of my Christian contacts in various European countries to help us find affordable accommodations, I worked with the American Express Travel Agency in Denver to book charter flights to Europe and purchase so-called Eurail passes which enabled our groups to travel economically on trains throughout Western Europe. We made several tours over four consecutive summers with groups from Del Norte and one trip with a group from the church in Estes Park. Groups averaged about thirty people and the countries we visited were in Northern, Western and Southern Europe, including Britain.

In conclusion I must say that my involvement in the life of this little community was intense and multi-layered. But the personal rewards in making friends and influencing many people with the Gospel of Christ were precious. When we left the little town we did so with heavy hearts. Never again were we to find as endearing a place filled with so many decent and caring people who were so open to the gospel, and who so much appreciated every effort I made to become more and more involved in their community.

The Lessons Learned: There is a distinction between "secular" and "sacred" work in function, but not in essence. Never be afraid to tackle assignments outside the church. As long as they do not impede your responsibilities as a pastor such activities, with the consent and approval of the church officers, may well contribute to a healthy growth of the church.

But a pastor is not just a "professional" required to help people with their daily lives, including the exciting leisure time activities described above, but he is also called upon to be their brother and friend in Christ. When a pastor makes friends in the church there is yet another benefit: The members of the congregation are also encouraged to make friends between themselves, and that can help their spiritual growth through a deeper caring and better harmony in the church. Finally, we read that even during the days of God's ancient people he reached out to Moses "as one speaks to a friend"(Exodus 33:11 NIV) and that "Abraham was called God's friend"(2. Chronicles.20:7 NIV). Let us then be friends with our flocks to better understand their needs, bear their burdens, and share their joyous expectations for eternity.

CHAPTER SIX

Common Sense Church Etiquette and Life Styles

The basic premise of every pastor and his congregation should be that any etiquette or the "delicate behavior patterns of the church" make common sense. Most churches I have served and visited struggle with the problems caused by continuity and change: For example, how to make the best of traditional and modern dress and behavior. Yet, amazingly there are many churches that develop attitudes and policies which go from one extreme to the other. While there are quite a number of areas that could be used as examples, I shall cite just a few of the ones I experienced during my ministry.

I shall begin with some observations about such common habits as the worshipers' appearance and deportment in the sanctuary. I have seen all the extremes going from the "ultra-formal" to the "far out casual." It is true of course that our culture has changed over the years and that the traditional formal attire for church attendance has given way to dressing much more casually. But "casual" should not mean "slovenly." Self-respect, respect for others and above all our awe and adoration for our Creator and Redeemer demand certain standards. While the definition of "casual dress" allows much laxity, tattered jeans, sloppy shorts, and immodest attire have no place in the sanctuary.

Another concern for many devoted Christians is the degree of noise that has become so common before worship services. The sanctuary is a place for meditation, adoration and praise of our heavenly Father, and not designed as a chatterbox for the latest trivia. Hearty greetings and friendly conversation should be enjoyed in the fellowship hall during coffee time, not in the place of worship. And while addressing the subject of excessive noise one might observe that the invitation of "making a joyful noise before the Lord" must always be in praise of Him. It is not a license for secular music no matter how much in vogue, whether classic or modern. It is wise for a well-planned worship service to observe the so-called "ACTS" rule that can also be applied to prayer: "Adoration, Confession, Thanksgiving and Supplication." I agree with the popular evangelist who once said that only music that specifically honors God should be heard in the sanctuary.

In what might be called perhaps a more important area of church policy there is the challenge of not just retaining visitors to the church but the urgent sense of pastoral responsibility to make sure that they have made a commitment to Christ. Most new faces in a church are seen during the Sunday worship services. This offers an excellent opportunity of getting to know these people better, and for them getting to know the church. I never ceased to be surprised at the missed opportunities that churches seem to be unaware of or indifferent toward when it comes to people who are visiting the church for the first time. It requires little intelligence to understand that whoever or whatever caused these newcomers to enter the sanctuary there is a good reason why they came.

Some pastors feel the urge to extend the so-called "altar calls" after the worship service to make sure that they don't miss anyone who has never confessed his or her sins to God and made a commitment to Christ. Altar calls are, of course, the standard practice for evangelistic services like the Billy Graham crusades and they work well for mass evangelism. Extending such challenges for an established congregation where the pastor presumably knows most of the people may not only be inappropriate but actually be perceived as offensive – unless the church service is held specifically for evangelistic outreach. The reason for this is obvious but evidently not always well understood: Most, if not all, members and visitors of an established congregation which enjoys a regular Christ-centered ministry do not need to be reminded – and, worse, confronted – with repeated challenges to repent and accept Christ as their Savior. To do so may imply that they never trusted God after making their first commitment, maybe many years ago and after extensive experience in worshipping the Lord and studying the Scriptures. Their primary need is not justification (being made righteous through Christ's redemption) but sanctification (growing in grace and knowledge of God).

Issuing a public challenge for people to come forward for evangelistic counselling after a worship service may be inappropriate for the regular worshipers, but at the same time there may be some people in the audience who desperately need Christ. It is therefore much better to extend an open invitation to meet with the pastor or other staff privately after the service in a hospitality room where the visitors are invited to learn more about the church – and their personal needs – in a relaxed atmosphere which may include some refreshments. It is important never to miss an opportunity to minister to a person in the full context of his or her need, but to do so with sensitivity and respect for their privacy.

From the very beginning of my ministry I made sure that no newcomer left the church "unrecognized" in the sense of not only being welcomed cordially during the service, but also greeted personally after the service. There are, of course, various tactics of doing that without embarrassing the person. Larger churches have a "welcome center" to which newcomers are invited as mentioned above, others have greeters from the congregation who engage the individual or the family in a conversation, some going so far as to invite them for lunch in a local restaurant.

Common sense demands that the pastor and congregation offer the best of hospitality to newcomers without coming on too strong. There is nothing worse than the conduct of some pastors – and more often church members – who merely tip their hats at new worshipers without any follow-up. Anyone who is serious about expanding the attendance, membership and influence of the church must cultivate and practice the habit of a sincere and hearty welcome to everyone who attends the worship service, especially to those who come for the first time.

Having made the argument for Christian hospitality, it is also important to understand its limitations. There are people who visit a church and for whom a hearty greeting at the door is sufficient. They prefer not to reveal their identity and their desire for privacy must be respected. That is why all overtures by the pastor and staff to get to know newcomers must be restrained and clearly show that an invitation is not an obligation but allowing the new worshiper to make the decision to what extent, if any, personal contact is desirable.

The second area of consideration is how to welcome pastors who are visiting from other churches or other parts of the country, and retired ministers regardless of their denomination. I have talked to a number of retired pastors like myself – after asking them to participate in the service perhaps by reading the Scriptures, saying a prayer or giving the benediction. The smiles on their faces said it all: They liked to be recognized and acknowledged, actively engaged in some small way in the worship service, and make a contribution in contrast to their unfortunately normal experience of being ignored or even shunned.

Being active in ministry even into my mid-eighties I have had no personal problems about feeling "useless," but other retired pastors have expressed to me feelings of disappointment when they were marginalized or even ignored, for reasons that completely escape me. Others have suggested that acting pastors may be too eager to guard their flock against what they perceive as "uncertified intruders" with questionable beliefs, or jealous of their reputations of being "Number One" in the church. There are allegedly even pastors who feel so insecure that they are suspicious of retired ministers in their midst of trying to usurp some kind of position and influence in the congregation, thus threatening their leadership. While this may sometimes be the case, any uncaring or indifferent demeanor of the pastor that fails to show the love of Christ and graciousness toward his colleagues portrays weaknesses in church etiquette that can diminish a congregation's effective witness for Christ and even inhibit church growth.

Another area of concern for the pastor is the role his wife may play in the church. I have been in some situations where the church leadership expected to hire two people for the price of one! There are two points to consider: The pastor's wife has an obligation to set an example of a devout Christian woman for the congregation. Further, her involvement in any church activity obviously depends on three factors: Family obligations, professional or other work commitments, and her desire to use her gifts for the service of the church. Let me say it here once and for all: A church leadership must never expect a pastor's wife to be active in any specific area of the church and, depending on her other obligations, apart from her presence for worship and prayer, she may not be active in the church at all.

However, in most cases the pastor's wife is more than willing to give some of her time and talent to the church, whether it is helping in the nursery, teaching a Sunday school class, or singing in the choir. I had a wife who wholeheartedly and with much dedication played the piano and conducted the choir in several of my pastorates – and that with six children at home!

To some extent the service of a pastor's wife depends on local circumstances such as a small church without many people qualified to serve, and on her natural gifts for the task. I have found that most pastors' wives make significant contributions to their husband's ministry in various ways, and they do so cheerfully and sometimes without much recognition for their work. But the extent of such service must be her and the pastor's decision. There should never been an expectation or pressure put on her to work in the church just because she is "the pastor's wife."

Further, in this chapter on church etiquette I would like to consider the subject of congregational responses to the pastor's ministry. There are, as always, ups and downs to this but I have found it very useful to have fellow Christians – and even those outside my faith – to monitor and evaluate my performance. One way of doing this is to have a question and suggestion box in the church where people can place comments and make recommendations that can help the pastor and leadership of the church promote and advance their ministry. Actually, I learned about this method as a college professor when, as chairman of the Department of History and Social Sciences, I required all of my professors (including myself) to submit to student evaluations, which were usually made after the end of the course.

This method may well raise a red flag for professors and pastors alike, but honest evaluations of my performance and effectiveness as a pastor and teacher have taught me much about myself, what I did right and where I went wrong, helping me identify my strengths and weaknesses, and giving responsible students an opportunity to voice their concerns.

Two examples of "evaluations," one from the pastorate and another from a large university – which can also apply to the church's teaching ministry - illustrate notable differences. In one of my churches where we had a "suggestion box" there were few noteworthy comments other than little notes saying something like "enjoyed the sermon," "we are glad you are here," "great preaching but too long," "I have problems understanding your accent," and, hilariously, "I really enjoy listening to your accent," the latter giving rise to concern whether the person listened to my accent instead of the message. There may also be complaints about the poor acoustics of the sanctuary, the excessive length of a communion service, insufficient nursery facilities, and so on.

The second example comes from the University of California (Irvine) and is mentioned here because I know that some pastors are also college teachers and may find this helpful. After teaching a class in Middle Eastern history and supervising the final examination, I handed out the usual course evaluation paper, which the students then passed on to the academic dean. Several days later in the dean's office I was told that I had an overall good evaluation, except for two students, a married couple, who contradicted just about every other student in my class by stating that they found my course "boring, repetitive, and uninformative." The dean smiled and suggested that I ignore the response – he certainly would. But rather than flatly rejecting an evaluation that seemed out of character with the others, I thought about it and wondered if there might not be some truth to it. After all, there is always room for self-improvement.

The bottom line is that a pastor or teacher should never be afraid of learning from his congregation or students, as the case may be. Evaluations, questions, suggestions and similar tools of testing can help our performance by correcting mistakes, sharpening our skills, and making us more effective in our profession as communicators.

Finally, a brief word about personal habits or more accurately the way they are expressed in our contemporary life styles. One must understand that, first of all, we cannot always judge people's faith by the way they live. Some habits and life styles are determined by cultural traditions. Others emerge from contemporary cultures that are viewed as trivial or worse by some, but they should never be condemned as long as they are not clearly mentioned in the Scriptures as sinful. Comments such as "he cannot be a Christian because he smokes cigarettes" are highly judgmental and may have nothing to do with the smoker's dedication to his faith, although it is commonly known that smoking is bad for one's health and friendly advice to quit is a good thing whenever it is appropriate.

I recall speaking at men's meeting in Alabama some years ago and, while sitting at the head table, the man sitting next to me pointed to a newly arriving guest with the words, "Charley is a great guy but he smokes his way to hell." The man talking to me was rotund with a big belly and at least 125 pounds overweight. If polluting one's lungs with tobacco smoke is not a commendable habit for a Christian, so is overeating or gluttony, but how many of us would pass the "obesity test?" Another example is the harsh criticism one hears today about tattoos and piercings, so popular among some of our young people. One could argue that it is wrong to try and improve what God has created, but it is also legalistic to look down on Christians who have chosen to look different. In my opinion this has nothing to do with a person's belief in the Christian gospel. In short, derogatory judgements about a person's appearance and habits can lead to false conclusions about his or her faith in God. Nobody is going to hell because he smokes cigarettes, wears a tattoo or, for that matter, drinks alcohol in moderation.

To bring these issues into sharper focus and make a more convincing case for them one only has to travel abroad and observe the life styles of Christians in other countries. For example, the evangelical organization of Torchbearers International frowns upon such habits as drinking alcohol in England, but the first item to arrive at the dinner table at their Spanish Conference center is a bottle of white wine! In Holland the elders of a Bible believing church drink a small cognac and smoke a cigar to the glory of God. In Germany there are few churches, including those who preach a "pure" Gospel, that do not serve a variety of wines at church dinners – as our travel group from Colorado was to find out much to their astonishment during a special welcome banquet organized by one of the churches we visited.

The Lessons Learned: A neat appearance and caring deportment showing discipline and the love of Christ are vital to the witness of the church. The sanctuary is a place of worship not loud conversation. The Church has a treasure trove of beautiful and inspiring music spanning centuries of musical genius. The practice of some "modern" churches to go into popular music that does not have a distinct Christian message fails in the pathos of their worship of our Mighty God.

New Testament Teaching encourages us to show hospitality to all strangers, but people visiting our church should not be strangers for any longer than they wish to be. Visiting pastors should be warmly welcomed as guests of honor and encouraged to participate in the church activities as deemed appropriate by the leaders of the church. The involvement of the pastor's wife in the work of the church must never been taken for granted but respected in the light of her natural gifts and her ability and willingness to serve.

Suggestion boxes and other means of evaluation can be useful tools of measuring performance and effectiveness. The feeling of discomfort of the preacher or teacher is a fair trade-off for knowing what the recipients of our messages, sermons or lectures are thinking about us, and using these means to improve our work. Finally, certain habits and life styles may not by themselves say anything about a person's faith. We must be careful to meet everybody with the love of Christ regardless of what they eat or drink or what they look like.

CHAPTER SEVEN

Giving to God: Tithes and Offerings

We are living in a world of material necessities. Money is the most common "medium of exchange" in most economies, and its desirability has led to an allure that has made "the love of it a root of all evil," (I.Tim.6:10 NIV). Yet throughout modern civilizations it has been used as a convenient means for buying, selling, and a host of other commercial activities. Christians and the church are not excluded from the ongoing need for money in order to accomplish their economic goals or, even more importantly, to ensure their continued existence and survival.

Before I go into the subject of proportionate giving, I have learned a few things about money and the ministry that have led me to write a word of caution. As I mentioned in the introduction, from the very beginning of my ministry God graciously gave me the wisdom never, under any circumstances, to be directly involved in church finances. The pastor may, preferably during a stewardship sermon, share with the congregation details of the church's financial needs, including appeals for special projects, but he must show careful restraint when talking about money. Detailed information about the church budget, including projections of income through tithes and offerings and appeals for special projects, especially if there is a budget shortfall, is best delivered by the church treasurer or other church officer entrusted with financial oversight.

It is also very important that annual budgets are drawn on realistic projections of income and expenses in order to avoid the common problem of local governments which, no matter how much money is raised through taxes, never have enough money to fund all of their cherished projects. My advice to budget committees has always been to identify and estimate the costs of all necessary obligations first, e.g., the pastor's salary and other expenses, utilities, regular church maintenance and mission giving, The pursuit or purchase of other "desirable" things like church vans for the elderly or a major renovation of the fellowship hall in the Pioneer Church of Del Norte, for example, were not part of the budget but launched and implemented through separate fund raising appeals. People would donate additional funds as they were able to, but the church's monthly obligations would never be put in jeopardy because no matter what happened the regular expenses of the church always took priority over any new project.

I have known churches that started ambitious renovation projects and suddenly were unable to meet their day by day expenses. This can happen when, for example, church members divert part of their giving to special projects at the expense of contributing to the regular budget. Stewardship education can help to guard against or even prevent that from happening, but if it does the congregation must be given to understand that the salaries of church personnel and supporting the local food bank are more important responsibilities than paving the parking lot. As for special projects, whether they may take two months or two years to accomplish them, time is less important than discerning God's will, even if it means that sometimes a project has to be postponed or even abandoned.

As a pastor I carefully avoided any handling of money, whether in the form of cash, checks or other financial instruments. I also made it a point to never check into an individual's giving habits or amounts, although I was sometimes apprised of major gifts to the church and the name of the donor. Least of all I would use the church's money to make payments to anybody. Writing checks, including those for my salary and other expenses, were always the responsibility and duty of the elected church treasurer or his assigned substitute if he was unable to handle a transaction.

Even quite recently I saw an example of a church in which the pastor was given responsibility for handling the finances. I simply shuddered when I learned of such a poor judgment of both the pastor and the leadership. Pastors carry their own burdens of sin and face all the moral perils common to every soul in their congregation. If the love of money is a cardinal sin, as the Bible teaches, it must be viewed with utmost caution and never should we allow financial dealings to cast any doubt on a pastor's honesty and integrity. I have known several pastors and heard of others who were forced to resign because of dubious or plainly dishonest appropriations of money that caused nothing but consternation and divisions in the church. Pastors face enough problems in the church that they cannot avoid. There is no reason whatsoever for them to get involved in the financial affairs of their church other than to pray that God will sustain their congregations financially as an extension and confirmation of His spiritual blessings.

An almost slavish dependence on the material commodity of money has led to conflicting interpretations of Biblical teaching as to what exactly God requires of a believer. In an amazing story recorded for us by Matthew the Pharisees tried to trick Jesus about the obligation of paying taxes. Jesus' reaction was swift and demolished whatever trickery these men whom he called "hypocrites" had in mind. After being given a coin with Caesar's portrait on it, He said to them: "Give to Caesar what is Caesar's, and to God what is God's," (chapter 22:21 NIV). That is a formula of giving not difficult to understand, and we can be sure that the taxpayers in those days, not unlike those of today, were left in no doubt not only about their obligation to pay taxes, but also how much they owed their government.

Jesus' comparison of our obligation to pay taxes to the government and to God, meaning essentially the church, establishes the fact, already based on the Old Testament law, that God expects us to share a part of our worldly possessions, like our money, with Him. In fact, the term "church tax" is used in some countries and sometimes even in our giving to churches that have no political connection. The key question is: How much does God expect us to give? This subject has led to a great deal of needless controversy due to the legal standards set in the Old Testament as opposed to the less stringent recommendations in the New Testament.

Let me begin to say that I never served a church that did not recommend tithing (10% of your cash income) and offerings (any gift to God that is not a tithe) as part of a stewardship program. This practice reflects the fact that many Christians believe that the Old Covenant (or Old Testament) requirement of tithing (based on the law) carried over into the New Covenant (or New Testament) which is based on grace. But many Christians struggle with the teaching that requires tithing and I was called upon more than once in my ministry to clarify the issue and lay to rest the conscience if sincere believers who wanted to do what the Lord requires of us.

Tithing in the Old Covenant was a requirement of the Law related to crop and cattle production, e.g., Leviticus 27:30, Numbers 18:26; 2.Chronicles 31:5. These tithes have been interpreted by some scholars as simply a tax for the priests who performed the sacrificial offerings. But there is no clear command for a legalistic tithing system anywhere in the teachings of the New Testament. When talking about giving to God there is no reference to the Old Testament Law of 10% or any other specific requirement for any amount of money, but the Apostle Paul encourages Christians to "give in keeping with their income: "Now about the collection for God's people: Do what I told the Galatian churches to do. On the first day of the week, each one of you should set aside a sum of money in keeping with his income, saving it up, so when I come no collections will have to be made,"(I. Cor. 16-1-2 NIV).

One can, of course, take the 10% figure from the Old Testament as a recommended minimum of giving to the Lord as many Christians do, but there is clearly no requirement to do so. It is important to understand that the New Testament teaches the importance of giving, but only in the form of a recommendation, not a demand. When reflecting on the difference between the theology of law and that of grace, this makes perfect sense. For the New Testament teaches that giving must come from the heart and performed in a spirit of joy – never as a divine expectation or a legal requirement.

All this implies that God sets no limits on giving – neither on the low end nor on the high end. I have had people in my congregations, and know other Christian friends, usually those whom the Lord has blessed financially, who give more than 10% of their income. A prosperous friend in Canada believes that 10% is merely the minimum that God expects, and that "real giving" starts after that. Others like him have given hundreds of thousands of dollars to church building funds and other projects, like helping countless individuals in need of a home or a car. And then there are those who struggle to throw a handful of coins into the offering plate because that is all the money they can afford to give away within the limitations of their income. They will ultimately earn the same praise from God as the poor widow mentioned in Luke who "put in two very small copper coins,"(21:2 NIV).

Ministers find themselves in a difficult position when they have to preach about giving and stewardship to their congregations. Holding the firm belief that I could never ask any fellow Christian to give more than I can based on a percentage figure, I could never urge a congregation to do what I could not do. But the real challenge really does not lie in the amount of a gift or in tithing 10%, but in a Christian's open-hearted willingness to give generously in proportion to his income, whatever God has laid upon his heart. Jesus reminds us of the corrupt nature of material wealth in Matthew (6: 19-21) concluding his remarks with the challenge that "where your treasure is, there your heart will be also," (v.21, NIV). In other words, not surprisingly, giving to God is more than a material transaction but an act of worship that has profound spiritual implications.

There are also other problems with a declared percentage of giving. In the Old Testament the money went to the priests of the tabernacle or temple. Does all of the tithe today go to our church, or do we divide the 10% for a benefit to various causes, organizations or even individuals outside the church? If there are unexpected pressing needs in our larger family, like a sister in law requiring urgent surgery she cannot afford, could a financial gift to her be part of our tithe? I believe that God would accept it as such. The problem with designed amounts or percentages is that nobody really has a formula for New Testament giving, but that it is a very personal and prayerful concern. While it is a matter of individual conscience and conviction to tithe or not to tithe, a percentile of 10% is relative and really depends on the amount of a person's income.

Worse, specific financial requirements for church members and even visitors, as the case may be, can actually exclude some people from a church. I met a young woman in Colombia, South America, who was struggling to raise a family on a very modest income. Her church demanded a specified amount of money every week as a "reasonable" offering. It was not much money by our standards, but she couldn't afford to pay the required amount and, too embarrassed to face the church officials, she never went back.

Proper money management by church officials is a vital part of Christian stewardship, which includes all we are and not only give. Because the church can only operate on the funds it receives from its members, adherents, visitors and friends, the leaders have a right to know how much a person is planning to give in order to set up a budget for the anticipated expenses of the church, just as the individual has a right to know what his or her annual income is in order to establish a household budget. This commitment, called "pledging," may not have the force of collecting taxes, but it enables the church board to set realistic goals for its necessary financial operations – and beyond that, as the case may be, for other projects that will require funding.

However, as with all the good things we can do for our church, even pledging can have a down side. Repeated announcements of collecting pledges, especially when made by the pastor, can elicit the negative perception often expressed by people who complain that all their church is doing is "asking for money." More fundamental to the problem of pledging, however, is the conviction of some Christians that their giving of money is between them and God – a highly private or even intimate - transaction which nobody else has a right to know.

Another problem, ironically, can arise when a large part of the church's budget comes from just a few major givers. While of great benefit to the pastor and his congregation and a tribute to their faith, major donors and generous regular givers in a church can discourage congregational giving, especially by people who hold a somewhat shallow view of Christian stewardship and might argue that "he has more money than I have, therefore my own giving is not that urgent." The doctrine of individual stewardship cannot be overemphasized as a transaction of faith between God and the believer regardless of what others in the church may contribute.

And then there is the perennial conflict between "financial security" and "living by faith." More than a theological issue, this debate is strongly illuminated by organizations that do not believe in pledging or, for that matter, making any public announcement or requesting endorsements for raising money so they can perform their mission.

The case of the "Children's Home and Mission" located in South Woodford, England, is a striking example. Founded by a Christian banker in 1899, it spread from a humble private home service for a few children into a child caring ministry the size of a whole city block. It touched and transformed the lives of hundreds of children over the years until more recently when the focus of this ministry shifted to the support of families in distress. Imagine being responsible for feeding, clothing, educating and showing the love of Christ to dozens of children at a time without a penny of regular income, and an adamant refusal to accept any commercial promotions to raise funds for this work. The obvious question then is: "How on earth did they manage to fund all of their expenses?" The answer: Entirely and exclusively through prayer. More specifically, the staff of a dozen or so Christin men and women would meet every morning and pray for the children's needs. And, yes, I must add that I had the immense privilege of attending some of those prayer meetings over the years. What follows is a very long story but it can be condensed with this simple statement: Never in my life have I experienced a more vivid sense of the reality of God and seen miracles of His providence that would shatter every form of skepticism and unbelief, and make many a Christian confront his lack of faith with deep shame.

The inevitable question emerges: Are we dealing with the same God even as most of us feel the need for a projected budget and pledges to support it, while others literally use fervent prayer to make food and drink fall out of heaven? Or have the times changed to the point that we now have become more "sophisticated" about meeting our financial needs? We already know the answer: Our Heavenly Father is "the same yesterday, today and forever" and He also as the Sovereign of the universe controls the dimension of time. He will answer our prayers today as He did a hundred years ago. God is not the problem – we are.

Finally, there is another aspect of giving that cannot be expressed by percentages, namely the numerous "free" services provided not only by the pastor but by members of his congregation. The evangelist Bill Graham, in an article entitled "The Time is Short," (Decision Magazine, June 2017, p.21) challenges his readers with this admonition: "Every Christian ought to tithe his money. But what about tithing your time?" One can only imagine the blessing God would pour out from Heaven if every Christian did that. Giving generously of our time can mean anything from a friendly service to personal sacrifice. What price is the pastor paying for the time and tears shed in the loneliness of his study after a tragic death or a difficult funeral? And of what value are the numerous services rendered in the church by men and women who love the Lord and give of their time and skills freely without a price tag?

The famous preacher and revivalist in eighteenth century England, John Wesley, who turned a whole nation back to God through his powerful preaching as was mentioned earlier in this book, was asked one day about the Christian duty of tithing. His answer encapsules for me the essence of all Christian economics. After thinking about it for a few moments Wesley smiled and reportedly said something like this: "Make all you can – Save all you can – Give all you can."

The Lessons Learned: Christians who pledge 10% of their income to God must always be respected and encouraged for their faithful stewardship. If every church member practiced tithing most churches would no longer have financial problems. However, tithing is a matter of personal conviction and reward. All giving from the heart is an act of worship and God knows how much money we can give and how much we are holding back. The New Testament writers call us for a commitment to giving according to our income, not for a specific amount. This means that tithing 10% may be considered generous, but the correct amount depends on our ability to give, and that may be less or even more. But tithing of our time, as Billy Graham rightly suggests, is another way of giving to God and for some of us perhaps the only way we can be generous toward the Lord.

One must never underestimate the element faith plays in how God provides for our material needs and remember that even tithing and pledging are merely guidelines for our material response to the Lord. Obviously, many things can happen in the course of time that would interfere with – and sometimes ruin – our best intentions and plans. It is the Apostle James who reminds us of the uncertainty of life with the challenge, "Now, listen you who say, 'Today or tomorrow we will go to this or that city, spend a year there, carry on business and make money.' Why, you do not even know what will happen tomorrow. What is your life? You are a mist that appears for a little while and then vanishes," (James 4:13-14 NIV).

CHAPTER EIGHT

Discrimination in the Church

Pope Gregory the Great (late sixth century) classified all sins under seven words which became known as "the seven deadly sins," – pride, anger, envy, impurity, gluttony, laziness and avarice, with pride being the most deadliest. That is true, of course, because it is pride that will keep men and women from God and so obviate their eternal salvation. Numerous Scriptural references confirm this, to quote one, "pride goes before destruction, a haughty spirit before a fall," (Proverbs 16:18 NIV). One might conclude from this that the sin of pride is a special target for caution and admonition in the church. That is certainly a message heard often either directly or implied, but the reality can be very different.

Let me say first of all that all of mankind is disposed to pride and one of its derivatives, discrimination, from the day one is born. We see this in every area of life – social, economic, intellectual, political, national, and even spiritual. For example, the Germans make jokes about the Poles, the Swedes about the Norwegians, the Danes about the Finns, and so on. The Scottish are convinced that they are better than the British, the British than the Irish, and the Irish than everybody else. But no form of pride has been more deadly than pride of race. From simple remarks designed to hurt an individual, the pride of discrimination has ignited violence and war throughout history. The Muslim Turks thought they were superior to the Armenian Christians and slaughtered almost a million people. The Nazis in Germany killed millions of Jews and other ethnic people in their perverted belief that Aryans were superior to all other races, committing one of the worst genocides in history. Not to be outdone the Socialists in Russia brutally exterminated even more millions for political reasons, and the Chinese during the "Great Leap Forward" indeed "forwarded" the death rate to history's all time high of an estimated forty million human beings who, in one way of another, dared to disagree with their revered "Chairman" for political reasons.

I have presented these historical facts to show that discrimination on account of race and religion, one of the most odious forms of pride, has made a ruinous impact on whole civilizations. It is then very disconcerting that we find an evil of such ugly proportions where one should never expect it: in the church. Pride of race is nothing new and has been a stain on American culture and in many other countries. What is surprising is that this evil managed to survive until modern times and, contrary to the political area where great advances in racial equality were made especially after the Second World War, it has still some vociferous advocates to this day in some churches.

The sin of pride, as mentioned above, can be seen in many places. But how about a place where men of the same race discriminate against each other on the basis of tribal differences? "Pride of Tribe" is not unusual in underdeveloped countries and there are to this day whole regions in Africa and elsewhere that succumb to this kind of discrimination..

During a visit to South Africa some years ago I had the opportunity to travel extensively with relatives who lived in the country and had first-hand knowledge of its politics and culture. During my month-long visit we toured the beautiful country and, among numerous other activities, I had the opportunity to preach in a church and visit two famous gold mines where we had an amazing and gratifying experience. After inspecting a mine down to its depth of 5,000 ft. (no wonder it was called "the Western Deep") the superintendent showed us the miners' living quarters. Apart from the fact that what we had already seen was quite contradictory to what the American Press consistently reported about this country in its usual derogatory terms of South African "apartheid," I was amazed at the spacious, clean and uncluttered houses occupied by the miners.

I was told that several dozen miners lived here and that the accommodations were divided by tribe, and for good reason: Coming from various parts of sub-Saharan Africa, these men clung to their tribal traditions and had to be separated from each other to keep peace and order. The superintendent explained that there was so much discrimination and bad feeling among them that even keeping them disciplined at work was no easy task. After visiting each house briefly and chatting with the polite but not overly friendly men, we arrived at the last house. After the superintendent knocked on the door, it was opened by a handsome black man with a big smile. This time we were warmly welcomed and after being invited to sit down we started a conversation. I noticed a Bible lying on a bookcase and, pleasantly surprised, I asked the young man what tribe occupied this house. He told us with obvious pride that all the men in this house were Christians and their unity in Christ superseded all tribal differences. It was one of the most gratifying experiences I had ever had, and I more fully appreciated the words of the hymn "In Christ there is no East or West, in Him no South or North, but one great fellowship of love throughout the whole wide earth" (Alexander Reinagle, 1836). Among these simple, hardworking and devout people in South Africa there was no room for tribal discrimination when they were united in the Christian faith and in their love for Christ. What a witness to the reality and love of God!

As mentioned above, pride has many ugly forms and can touch every part of life, including the social and economic areas. Although the Bible clearly warns us about the risk that material wealth can pose as a barrier between us and God (see Math.19:23-24) social and economic status can weigh heavily in some churches.

I experienced an example of that in one the few churches I served as a student pastor many years ago. Here the wealthiest man in town also "ran" the church, according to the words of one woman, "like a dictator," and also made sure that only men and women "of property" became church officers.

It was natural for him to look down on poor people, including students for the ministry who for the most part ranked among the poorest! Again, a steady, prayerful and uncompromising ministry of the Word combined with cultivating a Christian friendship with that man gradually led to an improvement of that situation. Eventually it had a more dramatic ending when the erstwhile "dictator" of the church became gravely ill and I prayed with him at his bedside in the hospital before he died of cancer.

As a fairly recent European immigrant to North America I had never encountered racial discrimination in a church until I moved to the American South which, generally speaking, I found to be very hospitable and a good area to raise a family. I had travelled extensively in the most of the Southern states in the course of various teaching and preaching missions and never encountered the specter of racial discrimination. But then I heard about a prominent church with a strong evangelical voice and an ambitious foreign missions program that, to my utter surprise, faced a situation it somehow failed to master because of racial prejudice in the church.

A man from the church expressed the problem of his church in a simple but powerful way with tears in his eyes showing his deep concern: "We're supporting missionaries serving in Africa, but our church refuses to minister to the black people in our own neighborhood." From all I knew about this church it was absolutely true to the Word of God, but in spite of its powerful ministry at home and abroad, it had failed to overcome and reject a social prejudice for which some areas in the South were still notorious.

The dispute about race had developed over some time when the issue was finally forced to a confrontation by one of the church officers. He had casually invited the black youths living in the vicinity to join in the activities of the youth group and afterwards to share refreshments with them. Although this raised some eyebrows the first, nothing was said about it. Emboldened he went a step further the following week and extended an official invitation to all of the youngsters living near the church to play and fellowship with the church youth. This time the reaction was swift and pointed: The call of a congregational meeting which failed to resolve the problem. Unwillingness to change church policy eventually led to the result that a sizable number of people, along with the pastor, left the church with its once bright witness for Christ now tarnished. It had fallen victim to its own unscriptural bias and policy of racial pride and discrimination that still had some vestiges in the Old South, including places where it was least expected.

The Lessons Learned: The story of the South African miners demonstrates our unity in Christ in a powerful way. If a group of Christian men from several underdeveloped countries can set aside their cultural differences in favor of a unified faith, it is shocking to find discrimination not only in our "civilized" society but even in the ranks of some churches. Social and economic pride can greatly hinder the work of God by curtailing church growth and the awareness and need for unity among believers. Any sentiment that seeks to diminish, downgrade, and ostracize people is derived from the sin of pride and contrary to the Bible's teaching. That includes discrimination on the basis of race, color or creed. Incredible as it appears to be, but even an evangelical, foreign mission focused church may stumble and fall for the deeply ingrained sins of pride and prejudice, serving as a caution and reminder of Scripture that "before his downfall a man's heart is proud,"(Proverbs 18:12, NIV).

CHAPTER NINE

The Challenge and Benefits of Multi-Tasking

Before I address this profound subject I need to mention the fact that multi-tasking does not work in every church, largely because the organization and some of the functions of the church changed when we entered the electronic age. We now have "mega-churches" that are a far cry from the relatively small community congregations and the pastors of large religious communities, often numbering in the thousands of members and worshipers, are of necessity very much tied to one major activity. They obviously do not have the time to shoulder many different tasks but must focus their ministry on teaching and preaching, especially if they use the electronic media of radio and television.

Many years ago while sitting across from Dr. James Kennedy during a personal lunch in Fort Lauderdale, he stated his regrets that he was unable to become more closely involved in the pastoral care of his large congregation. The challenging weekly task of preparing for a program known as "Evangelism Explosion," a popular radio and TV outreach program, simply left no time for a face-to-face pastoral ministry. In the light of these new realities my experiences and recommendations based on the lessons I have learned obviously do not apply to every pastorate, but that is a risk every author of a book like this must take. Commonality does not mean there are no exceptions and what may be typical in some areas can be exceptional in others.

But that is not the experience of most spiritual leaders. Many pastors would not be in the ministry today if they had not learned multi-tasking their time and talents early in their student careers. A pastorate with a relatively small membership can usually call a student minister to perform all the duties of a pastor and also leave him time to study, part time or full-time, as the situation demands. For most men and women this can present a formidable challenge, but with divine grace and an understanding congregation it can be a joyous experience. A student pastorate, unless the student works with a senior pastor in a specialized field like Christian education or the music program, is inevitably small in size for the obvious reason that the student must be able to divide his time between his studies and his pastoral responsibilities.

Most men and women who are called to the ministry or other Christian service understand that their main duties will be preaching and teaching the Word and celebrating the sacrament of Holy Communion as pointed out earlier. They also know that their work will include weddings and funerals, but they may be less aware of other tasks, such as home and hospital visitations, counselling, and involvement in the activities of other church organizations. Because these pastoral activities constitute the core of a pastor's ministry, I shall write a few comments about each in order to illuminate my experience and reinforce my conclusions noted in the "lessons learned."

Pastors may also serve other Christian organizations concurrent with their church ministry. Local and even nation-wide evangelism activities, for example, often require pastors with church positions to donate some of their time and talents to those ministries. This is what happened to me in Colorado and demonstrates that pastors may be called to a wider mission than their own churches. International Students Incorporated (ISI), located on Cheyenne Mountain Southwest of Colorado Springs, was such an organization and asked me to join their staff and work as their "in house" theologian on a part time basis. However, the more practical part of my mission there turned out to be face-to-face witnessing to foreign graduate students who were studying in the United States at various universities.

After arriving at the ISI facility one beautiful Saturday morning, the director asked me if I would speak to two of their married students from mainland China. I found them sitting in the shade of a big tree reading a Christian book. After introducing myself they told me that they were students at the University of Pennsylvania, from which I had also graduated. This curious fact seemed to forge a bond between us and their typical Chinese reticence with strangers quickly turned into smiling faces – and open ears! Both students, in their late twenties, were from Beijing and active members of the Communist Party. The young man was, in fact, a low level official in his part of town, and it became quickly clear that he and his wife were dedicated to their Party.

After relating my own story of growing up in the Nazi State, followed by a brief analysis of the yoke a totalitarian government places on its citizens, I told them how I met Christ in England, repented of sin and received Him as my Savior, and later devoted my life to the Christian ministry. After several hours of discussion interrupted by lunch and a worship service at the facility's main hall, we resumed our discussion. And then we prayed. It wasn't until the evening sun began to set behind the mountains that the couple accepted Christ as their Savior, and we embraced with tears of joy as brothers and sister in Christ. Indeed, pastors can also be evangelists and be given opportunities to share in the unique happiness of bringing the unsaved to Him – inside and outside the church.

A very different kind of pastoral duty is officiating at weddings for couples outside the church family. These joyous occasions of joining a man and a woman in matrimony are always a great honor and privilege, and they give the pastor a unique evangelistic opportunity. During the five years of my ministry in Del Norte I was asked to officiate at a number of these celebrations, and while some were considered "routine" in that they were held in our church, some were anything but. It was, of course, a very special joy and deep pleasure of performing the marriage ceremonies for four of my own children, my oldest son and three of my precious daughters. Two of these wedding were at our church in Del Norte, the other two on scenic mountain sides, one near the Continental Divide, the other outside the scenic town of Estes Park at Lily Lake. I was also invited to perform ceremonies on the summit of Del Norte Peak (11,000 feet); in a yacht club in Southern Alabama; in the far away forest wilderness of Oregon at the mouth of the Metolius River, and in an impressive mansion in San Luis Obispo, California, among others. Each of these ceremonies gave me the opportunity to present Christ to everybody who attended the wedding, and usually the response was gratifying.

The term "multi-tasking" applies to these events because some of the weddings were held in places far away from my church, some out of state, and therefore not a part of my regular ministry. But I saw my essential task as much the same in whatever I did and wherever I travelled: Representing Christ and reaching people in every walk of life with the Good News of His victory on the Cross as the answer to their "ultimate concern" in this life.

Some pastors are called upon to preach and teach beyond the religious setting of a church or mission hall. Evangelistic outreach often takes place at secular locations, some of them one might never think of. And so I found myself standing in the middle of a large hall preaching to the employees of a tire manufacturing plant in Scotland. I was supposed to have an audience of about 100 workers, but only a few were in sight. Most of them, too embarrassed to have "religion forked out to them" were hiding behind the pillars and partitions of the large hall, occasionally ducking out from behind their safe barricades to put a face on the voice they heard. I never heard what impact if any my speech made, but their manager advised me later that some folk in the hidden audience told him that they would "never forget that meeting," whatever that meant.

Another example comes from an outreach program sponsored by the ministerial alliance of Prince Edward Island. They had developed a plan for preaching the gospel in drive-in theaters where people remained seated in their cars during a worship service including music, prayer, and preaching from a platform equipped with powerful loudspeakers. After the service people were invited to gather with the ministers and Christian friends who attended the service for personal greetings and spiritual counselling. I spent about three months on Prince Edward Island and was invited to preach at the "drive in service" for four Sundays.

Preaching "to cars" was at first an unusual experience and I missed looking at faces that were expressing consent, approval, doubt or dismay, but I soon came to the conclusion that the gospel, when preached in the power of His spirit, has no barrier and even the invisibility of faces cannot prevent it from touching human hearts. Many of the Island's churches were involved in that "outside" ministry which reminded me of my student days in Scotland when teams of young Christians would go out on Sunday nights and engage in "open air" ministries.

There are some pastors whose deep concern for the welfare of their fellow human beings constrains them to engage in multi-tasking" of another nature. Their services are not marked by ambitious services, unusual projects or innovative ways to build up the church. Rather, they make themselves available to anyone who has a need – whatever that need might be, and they do it in the name of Christ.

An example of this comes from a pastor I met during my ministry on Prince Edward Island mentioned above. His name was Robert Bhe, the most gentle, humble and compassionate servant of God I have ever met. There was no favor or service too small, too "inconvenient" or too demanding that he refused to render: Taking people for medical appointments, to the hospital, helping them move, looking after their pets, helping them financially even from his limited resources, operating a food pantry, and being always available for anyone who expressed a need for prayer or counselling. I am including his humble ministry as an example of "multi-tasking" that certainly was not spectacular, but it demonstrates what, in fact, most members of a church could do for each other and what God expects from us as His servants.

Perhaps the most neglected area of a pastor's work is his ministry of prayer. All too often in the heat of battle we overlook the vital importance of constantly communicating with God, to "stay in touch" with our heavenly

Father Who initiates, directs, and eventually completes our calling. We are urged "to pray without ceasing" meaning that we should always be in a spirit of prayer, but I have never met a Christian man or woman who could claim that they "prayed enough" for the simple reason that even the most dedicated prayer warriors can never meet that challenge. Yet prayer can reward our faith like nothing else.

I have already mentioned the work of the Children's Home and Mission in London, England, in the chapter on "Giving to God" and how they operated their financial system entirely on the power of prayer. I simply want to repeat here that during my visits to that absolutely miraculous work for homeless children, I witnessed and heard of answers to prayer that brought the presence of God into my consciousness like nothing else.

Pastors are no strangers to sudden crises, tragic events that require sensitivity, fortitude, and superior personal skills. But they also experience joyous occasions when an outburst of prayers of intercession, pleas for comfort and hope, praise and thanksgiving rise before His throne of grace and find favor in His sight. A pastor will find that his effectiveness is measured not only by his human effort to provide faithful service to his congregation, but by his prayer life.

Pastoral counselling is another area of concern. Most pastors have had some training in crisis counselling as part of their seminary curriculum, but they soon find that such studies are inadequate for the vast variety of critical and complex situations they will have to face. Among the better known are premarital counselling and instilling hope in people who are overwhelmed by sorrow and grief for many different reasons, like an untimely death, a tragic divorce, or a major business failure.

I was fortunate to benefit from experiences with psychiatric patients in England, and later had the opportunity of improving my counseling skills by taking courses in pastoral psychiatry at the Provincial Hospital in Halifax, Nova Scotia. Throughout fifty years of ministry I never served a congregation where I did not find this training useful and effective for helping people and, almost as a by-product, expanding the church membership, because all ultimate comfort, reassurance and emotional equilibrium comes from God through His healing of our spirits.

Another area of pastoral duties and of frequently underrated importance is pastoral visitation, especially of the sick and elderly members of his church. Unfortunately, this is an activity that is rapidly being abandoned along with the home visits of caring physicians a long time ago. One may argue against the necessity of pastoral visits to the homes of the pastor's congregation by calling them "no longer necessary" because of the inconvenience they may cause to busy families who have other priorities (such as watching TV!), there is really no better way to reach people than in their own homes. By placing home visitation on my weekly agenda right after sermon preparation and teaching duties I quickly discovered that there is nothing more gratifying than showing the love of Christ through personal contact. I found that the ministry of faithfully preaching God's Word and the personal touch of the pastor as visitor is a winning method of attracting people's attention to our faith and our church.

Finally, this discussion is not complete without addressing the problem of time management. Effective multi-tasking requires the discipline of managing one's time in more than a casual manner. Even the most talented and energetic minister stands to benefit from watching the clock carefully, which is an important aspect of a busy ministry especially when we realize that the minister reports to no one but himself.

A pastor does well to recognize all of his talents, whatever they are, and then work them into time tables that optimize his work and performance. Many young pastors are well aware that their demanding theological studies could occupy all the time they have. But few can attend a seminary without other work to meet their financial obligations. Many students, in fact, are married with families and even the most generous scholarships usually do not provide enough funds to sustain a family without extra income. This compromise of time usually means delays in reaching one's goal of graduation from a seminary and subsequent ordination to the ministry.

There are many common denominators marking such a career, but each person's call to Christian service is unique, depending on numerous factors such as the individual's age, work experience, academic ability, education level, marital status and geographic location, among others. One of the best, perhaps the most ideal way, to train for the ministry is to become a student minister. Such a position helps not only with the student's financial needs by offering a rent-free house, a modest salary, and some reimbursable expenses, but it is an excellent training ground for serving a church full-time with expanded responsibilities in the future. But make no mistake about it, combining ambitious formal studies with a student pastorate requires a disciplined plan for time management.

My own call to serve the Lord had started as a full time ministry in the Shetlands, as noted, and later continued in a suburban church of the City of Saint John, Canada. But from then on I shared the experience of many young men who were training for the full-time ministry while serving mostly rural congregations located in the vicinity of the university or seminary where they were studying. At the time the Canadian Maritime Provinces (now better known as Atlantic Canada) had numerous unfilled vacancies of so-called "pastoral charges" that could include as many as three or four small rural congregations. Salaries were very modest, but the student pastor and his family usually had a rent-free home which was owned by the church, a travel allowance, and medical insurance for himself and his family.

A man looking at such opportunities faced a number of challenges, the biggest one being the reconciliation of his studies with his pastoral duties. This situation can be very demanding in terms of energy, diligence, and determination. Finding the time to do everything effectively can be a daunting challenge. But overall the system worked well for the student minister and his congregation. However, as might be expected, there were also potential problems. While there was usually a written agreement or contract that stated quite clearly what the church leadership expected of the young pastor in terms of his investment of time and effort, certain situations like emergencies could arise while the pastor was taking classes at the university and unavailable for urgent counselling, or asked to conduct a wedding or funeral at a time he had to take a college examination. A consensus is required that can sometimes test the good will of the church leaders and the young minister, something I had to learn over many years of student ministry in Canada and later in the United States.

This challenge of combining formal studies with serving a pastorate takes on a new face when the student is already ordained but working on advanced graduate degrees. Here a focus on the student pastor's special gifts can be helpful with his overall performance, but time can become a looming problem. Advanced academic programs tend to be much more demanding than undergraduate work and not everybody has the ability to master such tasks alongside other responsibilities. But a workable schedule can help a person cope with a volume of work that may otherwise not get the attention it deserves. I found myself in that situation while working on a doctorate and quickly learned that it required an optimum effort to cope with the sheer number of tasks and the never-ending stress of heavy workloads bearing down on me from all directions. At this point it is wise to remember the Biblical teaching that there are also times when God invites us to relax, like Jesus inviting his disciples to rest after they had returned from a strenuous time of teaching the crowds as recorded in Mark 6:31. There are many other passages that suggest that wise time management should not only cover activities but also much needed rest.

Doing post graduate studies, as mentioned above, can be particularly demanding on a pastor, but I can speak from personal experience and say, along with many other servants of God who pursued that goal, that it is quite possible. The following example demonstrates that I was able to manage such a career by the grace of God, who taught me that time can be as precious a gift as talent.

While serving the Presbyterian Church of Delhi in Cincinnati I studied at the University of Cincinnati, taught in the Medieval History department, served my congregation of about 200 members, made speeches to various organizations, preached in other local and some out-of-state churches, and finally, under the auspices of the Presbytery of Cincinnati, started a new congregation under the name of "St. Paul's Presbyterian Church" (later known as "The Bible Chapel of Delhi Hills"). I had indeed mastered the art of "multi-tasking" but I risked neglecting the needs of my family, which is a serious concern for any man in that situation. True, I was considered as having some "special gifts" to help me with my work and studies, but there was only so much time in a twenty-four day, and my family of a dedicated wife and six children did not get the attention they deserved – a problem that was to haunt me in later years.

Most pastors, of course, will never face professional challenges of such intensity. But especially in smaller churches the pastor may be called upon to fill a number of different roles and fulfill tasks that nay not require special talents, but that are necessary if he wants to meet the needs of his congregation. Teaching a Sunday school class, singing with the choir, helping elderly people with transportation, and even visiting relatives of church adherents who are facing special problems, all these and more are legitimate fields of a pastor's activities. You may find that such a display of Christian love in action will help you reach your people and others in the community more effectively than your best sermons from the pulpit. While it is true, as stated above, that a pastor cannot possibly fulfill all of his church's expectations, the more he is able to focus on the use of his special gifts and manages them in a timely fashion, the more fruitful his ministry is going to be.

I shall conclude my report about using my God-given abilities and determination to manage my time wisely while serving the Pioneer United Church in Del Norte, Colorado, mentioned previously in chapter 5 when dealing with a pastor's involvement in the community. Part of my need for multi-tasking stemmed from the fact that the small town of Del Norte lies at 7,800 ft. in the scenic San Luis Valley in relative isolation some 150 miles from the nearest major city. But the sincere, friendly, hardworking and honest people in this valley were a joy to serve as pastor. Their response to the gospel was heartening and over a period of several years the sanctuary was packed for Sunday services.

Being a small congregation in a small Western town a Pastor's resources were naturally limited, and I soon found myself busily involved in almost every aspect of church life. Apart from preaching and teaching I led the youth group, sang in the choir, and started a local travel program for the elderly. I engaged in a busy home visitation ministry and regularly visited the local hospital and nursing home. Two newly purchased vans, one for the youth group the other for the elderly, helped us with trips into the mountains, participate in events out of town, and build precious new friendships.

Finally, I must say a word caution about "multi-tasking." A pastor who makes himself eagerly available for any task at hand and becomes deeply involved in the work of his church does not always recognize the talents of others – and their need to use them for God's glory. No pastor can shoulder all of the tasks in a congregation and therefore he must learn to delegate. More important than his limitations, however, is the fact that God equips different people with different talents and their use for the task of kingdom building is expressed by the Apostle Paul when he teaches us that our unity in Christ as "one body" also challenges us to activate all of "our members." He goes on to write "we have different gifts, according to the grace given us" and then mentions the gifts of "prophesying, serving, teaching and giving generously" among others (Romans 12: 5-8 NIV). Pastors are obligated for the wholesomeness of the congregation and their more effective witness to the world to give the members of their congregation as much opportunity as possible to use their special talents. In his eagerness to do as much as possible he must be careful not to encroach on their desire and divine calling to contribute and to allow "the different members of one body" to work in unity for the glory of God.

The Lessons Learned: Performing a variety of tasks can enrich a pastor's experience beyond any additional financial rewards. This is true inside and outside the church he is serving. A versatility in the duties performed and increasing the scope of outreach and involvement in other organizations can also be a real blessing to the pastor and his congregation. But multi-tasking begins at home with the many tasks a pastor must fulfill. Also, some of the most rewarding responses to the gospel may come not as the result of a sermon after a worship service, but on a quiet mountainside.

But time management, I repeat, is a vital component of multi-tasking. Without it one cannot expect a successful dynamic of success even in routine tasks, like sickness visitation, not to mention big projects like international tours. Our time like our talents, are a vital part of our stewardship and commitment to the Lord.

The author with his first family

Silver Falls United Church, Canada - Old and New

The author with his wife Sofia and daughter Laura

The author with his wife Sofia in Florida

The author giving one of his many lectures and speeches

Heller's Angels on Imogene Pass (13,114 feet)

CHAPTER TEN

Tent-Making to build a "House not made with Hands"

The Apostle Paul was known to be a "tent maker," a Biblical term later used for a pastor or any Christian worker who makes or subsidizes his income from "secular" work outside of his spiritual mission. That did not mean that Paul would not receive gifts from churches as is evident from his gratitude for the material assistance some congregations gave him during his ministry. But Paul chose not to rely entirely upon having all of his material needs met by the congregations he served. Instead he worked with his hands to support himself in the time honored trade of tent-making.

We don't know exactly what his reasons were, apart from seeking some economic independence, for this activity outside of his teaching and preaching career as an Apostle of Christ, but his activities gave sanction to others, including myself, who decided to pursue a similar path of earning a living. My reasons for this I explained in the introduction of this book, and few people have ever questioned them.

When discussing a tent making ministry one must begin with the obvious question: Are my "extracurricular" activities in conflict with my call and obligation to contractual agreements? It would be a denial of economic fairness and serious breach of conduct for a pastor if he received a full salary with the expectation of devoting all of his time to his church, and then take an outside job unless there are good reasons for doing so and his activities are supported and approved by the church officers.

The best scenario for a tent making ministry is to be free of any contractual duties with a religious organization and maintain an itinerant ministry of teaching and preaching as the Lord leads. I did this for years and the Lord blessed that work. However, if an itinerant ministry isn't an option for the pastor and he has a congregation that accepts work outside the church this is certainly acceptable as long as those activities are not an impediment do the growth of the church. During new church development when there are often not sufficient funds to cover the minister's expenses, that can pose a real challenge and lead to doubtful expectations about a rapid expansion of the new congregation. Tent making, such as college teaching, is also possible when the pastor is part of a team of ministers of a larger church with shared responsibilities.

The Del Norte church, for example, not only suggested that I teach part-time at the high school, they also encouraged me to engage in the business of real estate to provide extra income for our family of eight. None of these activities seemed to diminish my preaching and pastoral care ministry in the church, but it also meant that it required an extraordinary amount of energy and determination to get everything done.

Perhaps the most amazing example of combining teaching, preaching and business activities comes from my work in Chattanooga, Tennessee. After my first year as chairman of the Department of History and Social Sciences at Covenant College, I served as Assistant Pastor at the Westminster Church, worked some evenings as an efficiency expert at the Master's Carpet Corporation, and almost every Sunday filled the pulpit in other churches that had a pastoral vacancy. Some of these congregations were located at a considerable distance from home and required hours of travel. In other words, even when my pastoral appointments were considered "more than part-time" God enabled me to perform additional tasks, but I never did so without affirming His will by obtaining the gracious permission of my employers to whom I was accountable how I spent my time.

While teaching at Taylor University in Indiana I also served a small church in nearby Jonesboro, activities I enjoyed very much. But my allergies, both hay fever and asthma, became steadily worse. As time went by one of my daughters, who also suffered severely from allergies, had to increase the dosages of powerful cortisone drugs and medical wisdom dictated that we had to find another part of the country which was free of the dreaded ragweed pollen. These allergies, along with some other reasons, prompted us eventually to move to Colorado, a State virtually free from the ragweed and delivering the pollen free air we both needed.

There are always those who are critical of pastors who earn money outside the church regardless of the reasons, sometimes pointing to I.Tim. 6:10 where the Apostle Paul warns us that "the love of money is a root of all evil." He goes on to say that "some people, eager for money, have wandered from the faith..." The lust for money manifests itself in our society as unparalleled greed almost anywhere one looks. Because it is a seductive and dangerous detraction from spiritual things, money has always been a major idol of worship. However, this does not mean that it is necessarily wrong to make money and even to seek wealth. While there are many people who have made money indeed as their major purpose for living and forfeited divine salvation of their souls because of it, others have used their wealth to be a major influence for Christ and embarked on missions of charity the average wage earner could only dream about. Money is not an evil in itself, but actually can be a blessing depending on how it is used. Unfortunately, we all know of churches that are not only focused on raising money but also known to be extravagant in its use, like the preacher who insisted that only the purchase of a multi-million dollar jet airplane could fulfill his self-defined ministry, or the TV evangelists who build multi-million dollar mansions "for the glory of God."

But there are also churches that raise money outside the bounds of congregational tithing and other charitable giving. The following example is perhaps one of the most curious and humorous though understandably not without its critics. It comes from a rural pastoral charge in Nova Scotia that at the time had a student pastor I got to know well as we often shared a ride to our theological seminary in Halifax. The background to this story was a custom of rural churches to sponsor a "Strawberry Festival" once a year to raise money for church expenses. These were well planned events and the ladies of the churches were busy sewing and knitting garments and baking cookies and cakes, while others used their artistic abilities to make a variety of products for sale to the public along with serving delicious strawberry dishes. These events were so well attended and financially productive that the income derived from them often constituted a major part of the student pastor's annual salary. But as the following story will show, sometimes the zeal for these events may have gone a bit too far!

While discussing our plans for the next Strawberry festival, my fellow student pastor began to grin from one ear to the other and told me of his congregation's truly "innovative" plan to make a lot of money. They were going to engage the services of two female wrestlers from Halifax who also happened to be elders in his church. I almost crashed the car with shock and laughter, but my friend confirmed what I had just heard, adding that they were going to make "a lot of money." In that he was true. When I saw him again the following week and asked him about this bizarre event, he boasted that people had come from all over rural Nova Scotia to watch their female wrestling show, and that his church had made more money than ever before.

Needless to say, in the course of their daily duties pastors need money to meet unforeseen expenses often for charitable gifts to destitute and sometimes even desperate people. While I strongly discourage pastors from handling church funds, they should be entrusted with some money to help the needy at their discretion but also give a monthly account of that spending.

Perhaps the greatest satisfaction of a tent making ministry apart from generating extra income is the enjoyment of relative freedom from the rigid time table of routine activities that are much less a part of an itinerant ministry. Ironic as it may sound, I felt a greater sense of freedom when I engaged in several different activities such as college teaching and business consulting combined with serving a church than when I served a congregation full-time.

There were few Sundays when I did not find myself in a pulpit, but the telephone never stopped ringing with invitations to speak at numerous meetings of churches and other organizations covering a wide spectrum of public service from religious retreats to civic and political organizations. In fact, during some of my time in Cincinnati I had the somewhat unusual experience of doubling up on nightly speaking engagements, scheduling some for dinner meetings around six pm followed by other meetings later that same evening. Although I never stated a fee for my activities, God provided generously to support our family of eight

The Lessons Learned: Always strive for the optimum fulfillment of your God-given talents no matter where such a challenge takes you. Make as much money as you honestly can, but beware of its dangerous allure and the temptations it may offer. Never be afraid to walk through an open door of opportunity to serve Christ. But be careful that too many activities can also lead to problems in your marriage and family as I found out to my bitter regret and which I shall detail in another chapter. But by carefully focusing your thoughts on God's will, and with constant prayer for His guidance, you will always find new ways and places where you can be a messenger of the Good News. Again, money well spent can be a great blessing for your ministry but always use it with prayerful Christian stewardship.

CHAPTER ELEVEN

The Pastor and his Relationship to Church Government

Most historic churches, unlike non-denominational congregations, have a tiered structure of government within which the local church and its pastor must operate. This is obviously not the place to examine the numerous types and functions of church governments, but a few paragraphs are relevant to the subject of this book.

My own experience with church organization during my ministry over five decades is limited to the Presbyterian system of government. Some people think, and I agree with some justification, that the Presbyterian form of government is the most democratic of all Christian denominations. They begin with the local church, a city or an area-wide organization called the "Presbytery," a regional entity known as the "Synod," and a national body called the "General Assembly." This is not meant to be an authoritarian structure like the hierarchical organization of the Roman Catholic Church and some other Protestant churches, but ideally functions to promote the goals and welfare of the whole membership of the denomination. Because divisions in the church are just as common and unfortunate as in other organizations, one can expect disputes and disagreements on all levels of the church. But its overall mission purpose, whether defined as mostly spiritual or social, is usually well accomplished unless there are major contests of important doctrinal or ethical matters for which the church, unfortunately, is also sometimes notorious.

In the Presbyterian Church, as mentioned elsewhere, the local congregation is supervised by the ruling elders known as "the session" who work closely with the pastor who is also known as a "teaching elder." A Board of Deacons is entrusted with caring for the worldly needs of the congregation, and the Trustees are charged with the responsibility of managing the financial and building affairs of the church. This is seen by many as a Biblical model of church management and, in my experience, has worked well in the churches I have served.

Conflicts arise when disagreements deteriorate into "church politics" and when a consensus for doing what is right in the minds of the majority is compromised. Even more serious is a dispute over basic church doctrine, and that happened in the church I served in Lamar, Colorado. It was one of the very few times I found myself in the middle of a major doctrinal contest, and the nature of it is noteworthy.

A small group of Pentecostal families in the congregation demanded the teaching of certain gifts they believed to be essential for a person to be a "true believer," which is sometimes expressed by the term of having a "second blessing." Examples of this are the gift of "speaking in tongues," the ability of physical healing and other abilities endowed to us by the Holy Spirit mentioned in the New Testament. Presbyterians do not deny that some Christians have these gifts although the Biblical reference to "speaking in tongues" is by most Reformed scholars interpreted as "languages." But they differ from some Pentecostals in that they do not consider them as essential for personal salvation and, therefore, they are not part of Presbyterian Reformed doctrine. This fact made the demand for Pentecostal theology inappropriate, and our Session supported my recommendation that these very dear and well-meaning people find another place of worship. The Presbytery Committee on church doctrine was called into the situation and confirmed our joint proposal for a peaceful departure of our Pentecostal brothers and sisters for preserving the peace of our church. They departed for their chosen place of worship without further problems which effectively resolved the matter.

Every pastor will occasionally experience problems with the church leadership, usually about the programs of the church and perhaps some differences about the fine points of church doctrine. However, I can say that I have never had a problem or an issue with one of my Sessions that we could resolve through prayer and Christian love – even if the pastor was not always right on every issue!

Shortly before I left Indiana for Colorado, the Pastoral Ethics Committee of the Presbytery in which I was serving had to deal with a difficult case concerning a pastor's marriage. He wanted to divorce his wife in order to marry another, much younger woman. His wife refused a divorce and, to the committee's utter surprise, the pastor presented the woman he wanted to marry at one of our meetings, obviously hoping that by this action we would be more sympathetic to his cause. But the committee, after much debate and heart-searching, unanimously decided that without the pastor showing any desire or intention to resolve his marital problems through prayer and discussions with his spouse, it would support his Session's recommendation to ask him to resign unless he showed a change of heart and agreed to marital counselling.

I am relating this story because behind the cold facts there was much emotion in the committee. The "tears shed" in this little desert of distress came from men who were very much aware of their own weakness, and a warm stream of sympathy went out to both the pastor and his wife. It was an example showing that pastors can expect demands on their ability to make difficult decisions as they have the future career of one of their own in their hands. Rendering justice without being judgmental is not an easy task, but it can be a very real part of a pastor's ministry.

I might add here the sad but true fact that sometimes pastors fail morally just like other Christians. They are not towers of moral strength but, in spite of their calling and position, just as susceptible to deviating from the Biblical norms of morality as anyone else. However, because of their spiritual leadership qualities people expect, justifiably, more from them than from any other church member. They tend to overlook the reality that a pastor is in God's sight no more and no less than a forgiven sinner like everybody else who claims to be a Christian.

The Lessons Learned: As the case may be, the pastor would do well to remember that he is part of a greater organization than his local church, and that there are resources available to help him in cases of theological and moral dispute. Also, a pastor's ministry is often wider than his local congregation, and he must be prepared to give of his time, talent and emotional capital when it is required for the benefit of the greater communion of saints. In my experience one is never far enough removed not to be affected by the problems faced not only by members of his congregation and community, but by other servants of God who have stumbled and failed in their commitment to serve Him.

CHAPTER TWELVE

Tragedy in the Church

All of life is in a constant state of crisis and tragedies are a part of it. But the stress that is generated by the many vicissitudes of life, ranging from joy and peace to sorrow and conflict, find a major focal point in the church. It is the only institution on earth that deals with what the theologian Paul Tillich called "ultimate concern" (pondering our fate after we die) which he distinguishes from our "immediate concern" (our cares in this world). In other words, this is the natural worry experienced by every human being concerning the eternal fate of his soul in contrast to his daily preoccupations of meeting the demands and surviving the challenges of his earthly existence. The pastor then is called upon to minister to both concerns: Life in this world and the anticipation of eternal life after death.

Going back to the German word *"Seelsorger"* (a person who cares for the needs of the soul) we see that the main purpose of the church is to lead sinners to salvation by accepting the sacrifice of Christ on the cross, and to eternal life as the "second fruits" of His resurrection. That glorious event is preceded, of course, by the tragedy of man's physical death. But the Biblical message is quite clear that we can reach the unsaved by obeying Jesus' commands that we also minister to the bodily needs of our fellow citizens as a "labor of love." This is often the pathway to reaching a lost soul.

All this appears to be simple enough, but there has been an age-old conflict in the church over the priority of the two major life concerns defined by Paul Tilloch in his theology as "immediate and ultimate concern" as stated above. Contradictory as it may seem, one finds that a large part of Christendom prefers to put the emphasis on "immediate concern" and considers the Biblical answer to man's "ultimate concern" as a mere after thought. There are many reasons for this, but it is not my purpose to delve into one of the most profound and debated problems the church has faced throughout its existence.

There is, however, one stark reality nobody can ignore: What is the message of comfort and hope the pastor or priest has when he stands above an open grave? All of the well-meant and surely important work for the welfare of physical existence are suddenly irrelevant because at stake is the eternal fate of the soul even as the body is gone. When pain, illness and death strike, all of our "good works" designed to help with our "immediate concerns" are not sufficient to save one single soul. Temporal welfare for the body has triumphed over eternal life for the soul. Sadly, that is the truth emerging today from some of our major denominations. It was also the sin of the Roman Catholic Church in the sixteenth century which the Reformer Martin Luther denounced with conviction to the point of contempt. Mankind has perennially suffered from a tension between their concerns for the here and now and for the beyond, with an inclination to live life as if eternity does not exist. But not always: The brutal realities of decay and death are warnings of impending peril that nobody can escape. A true "Seelsorger" is keenly aware of them because they control the heartbeat of his mission and the passion of his ministry.

When disaster strikes the immediacy of God's spiritual message hits us harder than at any other time, and woe unto the pastor who is not prepared for the ultimate realities of life. The challenge before him is to master a deep compassion and sadness with a degree of control and calm that he can only draw from his faith. It is something one cannot learn in seminary but comes gradually through the testing to which he will be subjected during each crisis event. One thing is certain: Every special event in life, whether it is a joyous wedding or a tragic death offers a God-given opportunity to challenge those affected to making a commitment to Christ, because there is no better opportunity to remind them that there is a God in control of everything. Serious illness and death are grim reminders of our ultimate concern when people focus on the hereafter, and I have found that most people will listen attentively to the Christian message that offers salvation and eternal life in Christ, and that they have "an eternal hope in the heavens,"

Funerals can have their problems but also present unique opportunities for witnessing to "the hope of our calling" with the Biblical assurance that those who die in Christ inherit newness of life and that "nothing shall separate us from the love of Christ" because we are "more than conquerors through him who loved us," (Rom. 8:35, 37 NIV). During a funeral sermon the pastor lays his sensitivity, compassion, and faith in God's mercy on the line. In fact, many people will judge the effectiveness of their pastor by his funeral sermons because he is, after all, addressing the ultimate concerns of the bereaved and others in the audience.

This is a time for contemplating the transiency of physical life and the soul's eternal destiny. It is a unique opportunity for the pastor to contrast the superficiality of this life with the profundity of the life to come, and to remind his congregation that life is essentially divided into life on earth or life in eternity with or without Christ as mentioned earlier. It is now that people must be led to realize without a doubt that the decaying body, like a kernel of wheat in the ground, must die in order to bring forth new life. As the Apostle Paul put it so reassuringly when writing to the church in Thessalonica, "Brothers, we do not want you to be ignorant of those who fall asleep, or to grieve like the rest of men who have no hope. We believe that Jesus died and rose again and so we believe that God will bring with Jesus those who have fallen asleep in him," (I. Thessalonians. 4:13-14 NIV). His statement concerning "men who have no hope" is absolutely terrifying and reminds us that only those who have faith in Christ and their sins forgiven will go to heaven. I am deeply convinced that this passage is more often misrepresented at funeral services than any other except for a reference to the inheritance of eternal life which is dubious when the deceased has left no record or indication that he or she trusted Christ for salvation. Even in doing his best to reassure the family and other loved ones of the dead person, a pastor must be careful never to distort the truth by offering a false hope. When the pastor stands at the grave side uttering the traditional words "earth to earth, ashes to ashes, dust to dust in the sure hope of the resurrection to eternal life" he'd better be speaking from knowledge of the deceased and his conviction that he is referring to a born-gain Christian and not to someone who, at best, never made a commitment to Christ as Savior or, at worst, openly repudiated the Christian faith. We all know that ultimately only God knows a person's heart and status before Him. But Jesus told us that "by their fruits you will recognize them" (Math. 7:16 NIV) and it is usually not too difficult to identify a true believer from a merely "religious" person or, worse, an unbeliever. If the pastor never met the deceased and learned nothing about him from others, he should be very careful not to make promises at the grave that were never inherited by the deceased during his life in the flesh. One can still offer hope assuming the best, but there can be no finality about it. This is not a matter of being legalistic but realistic and faithful to God's truth. It is in Him that we must put our trust during difficult times like these.

Here than is a word of caution worth repeating. Most pastors are greatly tempted, in the name of propriety and comforting the mourners, to preach as if everybody, believers and pagans alike, share in the triumph of Jesus' resurrection. Tragedies in a church can have many faces, but they can be divided as spiritual and physical. One of the greatest spiritual crises in the church is caused by the notion that somehow "good works" are an acceptable substitute for saving faith in Christ when they should be a result of such faith. The Apostle Paul clearly draws the line between those who have faith and those who have no hope by stating that "we are saved…through faith… not works," (Eph. 2:8-9 NIV). What a chilling statement of ultimate truth, and how dishonesty triumphs when it is ignored or by-passed in the name of a false and deadly universalism. The Gospel message, in a sense, is only "good news" for those who repent and always draws a clear distinction between those "who die in Christ" and those who reject Him. This brings us to the physical crisis of death. A funeral, as an example, should never be a time to distort that fundamental truth about our faith, even if it means "offending" people who believe otherwise.

Very early in my ministry God gave me a deep empathy for those who mourned the loss of family and friends. May be the spectacle of death all around me during the Second World War in my home town of Hamburg had made me extra sensitive to the pain felt by people who had lost loved ones. I will never know, but after conducting several funeral services in Nova Scotia the funeral director offered me a full time position as funeral chaplain in his company. A few years later I was offered a similar position in Cincinnati, Ohio, but I declined both of them because I had plans to teach at a Christian college and preach in whatever church invited me. I have officiated at numerous funerals throughout my ministry, but some really tragic ones stand out in my memory and have contributed to whatever "wisdom" I have been able to gather over the years.

In my Cincinnati church we had a father and son who enjoyed one of those special relationships one does not see very often. Both felt clearly attracted to my evangelical ministry and it was a deep joy for me to see them in church and chat with them afterwards. I soon found out that the father loved his son very deeply because the sixteen-year old boy had a serious medical condition and his father was deadly afraid of losing him. I learned all about his illness and the prognosis during a visit to their home. The son had liver cancer and they were planning for a delicate operation. I left after fervent prayer and a week later I had a call from the father that his son had died during surgery. It was another sad event in the church and people came from all over the area to offer their condolences, but the father was nowhere to be found.

There followed a difficult counselling ministry later with a grief-stricken man who could not accept that God had taken away his beloved son. I shared with him again the story of Jesus, God's own son, and how he had sacrificed Him for our sins. It was a long process but eventually the man came back to church. I believe that the story of the Cross ultimately gave him the comfort and peace he was seeking after his tragic loss. Yes, funerals remembering the dead can break down human pride and lead to a unique sense of reassurance for the living.

Among some of my most fragrant and painful memories is the story of a young couple who worshiped with us in Newport, Nova Scotia. They were in their mid- twenties and very much in love with each other. Mature Christians for their age, their presence lit up the worship service and both of them became very popular in the community. It was with great joy that I performed their wedding ceremony, taking away the feeling that the two were truly made for each other.

A short time after the wedding, tragedy struck. In the middle of the night I had a telephone call from the young woman, who informed me with a grief stricken voice that her beloved husband had died of a heart attack just a short time ago. After my arrival at their home I found the young wife overcome with grief and as we prayed kneeling down beside each other it took all of my self-control to keep my voice steady. But, as always, I found that during our darkest hours the light of Jesus Christ shines the brightest in the gloom. After the grieving wife had recovered somewhat from her shock I assured her that her beloved husband was now free from all pain and home with his Savior. The whole town came out for the young man's funeral and after the brief message of comfort I made my usual challenge: This wonderful young man has gone prematurely, but safely home. Do you know where you are going?

Among the numerous funeral services I conducted over the decades I had a somewhat similar experience in the San Luis Valley. Our motor cycle group rode the high country of Colorado for many years, and by the grace of God we only had a few minor accidents during that time. But that was tragically changed when a deadly accident happened, not during one of our group rides, but when a friend and fellow rider from Alamosa was out in the mountains enjoying his bike with a fellow rider in the heavily forested Del Norte Peak area. Riding around a corner on a lonely forest road at a relatively high speed he ran head-on into a logging truck and lost his life. It was a great tragedy for us all and, as always, the whole community was in shock. About one year before the accident I had performed this young man's wedding to a lovely young lady who now came to me with the inevitable question: Why? A few days later I found myself standing before her and more or less the same crowd of people, first in the pulpit and later at the open grave, burying a man who had always delighted our group with his cheerful presence. Yes, the tears in the desert flowed afterwards.

Sometimes a funeral service is a very personal affair when, for example, it involves a close family friend, a child, or someone in your own family. I was returning from Mount Allison University located in Sackville, New Brunswick, to my church and home in Dorchester, a twenty minute drive. Just a short distance from my home a large crowd had gathered. Young Edward Duffy, our neighbor's son just 11 years old, had been struck by a car while riding his bicycle and people were waiting for the ambulance. By the time the medics arrived the boy was dead. Edward and my oldest son were the best of friends and shared many play times together. On other occasions we welcomed young Edward to our table for lunch or dinner. I was overwhelmed with grief and tears, and shuttered at the test before me: his funeral. Edward's grief-stricken parents asked me to conduct their son's funeral within three days of his death. That would be Easter Sunday, 1960. After many hours spent in grief counselling the day arrived. The church was packed as I sat in the study overcome with sorrow and trying to ponder the message I had prepared. I was shaken to the core of my being and trembled as I got up to walk into the sanctuary. I cried out silently to the Lord, "Please, give me strength, I can't do this by myself." And then I felt a surge of energy, an emotional lift go through me and walked on to faced one of the saddest crowds I had ever seen in my life. I spoke the words God had laid on my heart and, before the internment at the cemetery, prayed for a while in my study while the tears flowed. Hundreds of mourners still sitting or leaving the church did nothing to change my feelings of deep sadness and compassion for parents who had lost their young son. I also discovered again that God speaks to His servants in times of crisis. I was not the first pastor to realize that for those whose hearts are open to the working of His Spirit, it is through sadness, grief and sorrow that we come to know more clearly the comforting reality of our gracious heavenly Father.

The Lessons Learned: It is in his primary role as a "Seelsorger" that a pastor finds himself at the very core of life's most traumatic events. In a sense all of his messages from the pulpit must, in some way, come together and contribute to the inescapable reality that "a man is destined to die once, and after that to face judgment," (Hebrews 9:27 NIV).

CHAPTER 13

Going Forward: New Church Development

There is arguably nothing more rewarding for a pastor than starting a new congregation or building a new sanctuary. The difficulties of these tasks are well worth the reward. They often provide a unique sense of calling and accomplishment as the pastor participates in yet another step of kingdom building. But any expansion project must be prepared with much prayer and a vision of the pastor and congregation making sure that this is really what God has laid upon their hearts. Sometimes new churches are built in anticipation of the need for a larger place of worship, and at other times a denomination may build a new church in the hope that a strong preaching and pastoral care ministry will attract people from the community to attend and support it. Depending on the local situation these may be good reasons for church expansion as long as the need of the people precedes any ambition of building a new sanctuary.

I had never entertained the idea of getting involved in new church development, but was surprised to find myself at the center of it after serving the church in Silver Falls, New Brunswick, for a just few months, as previously mentioned in another context. There are various methods of starting a church, whether it is with a new congregation or a new building to meet the needs of an expanding membership. It is quite natural to look at an area in the city or in a village where there is no visible place of worship and go in with the gospel. It is also a practical matter to think of a new sanctuary when the old one is too small or no longer adequate for public worship or other reasons. Finally, there are areas that either do not have a place of worship or lack a church of a certain denomination.

Church expansion is another example of "new church development" except that we are talking now about an established church that was in a state of decline in terms of attendance and support. This was the case, as mentioned above, during my very first ministry in Canada after arriving in New Brunswick from England on a bitterly cold November morning. For reasons I never understood the Silver Falls United Church had seen a sharp decline in attendance over several years and prior to my arrival there was actually some talk at Presbytery level of closing the church. The decision to call a student pastor all the way from England was seen by most of the few worshipers left as a last desperate measure to save the institution. In any case, I knew after talking with the elders that the answer to such a situation is obvious: Start preaching the saving gospel of Christ, the joy and peace of Christian living including the cost of discipleship, and get to know as many people personally as possible through a rigorous program of pastoral visitation. While unsure of the extent, I had already learned that God had given me two special gifts for such a task: the gift of oratory and personal skills.

Within a few months church attendance went from a handful of people to an overflow crowd requiring folding chairs down the aisles as I experienced with deep joy the sound of the "crunching wheels" made by car after car arriving and parking on the graveled parking lot. I left the church ten months later to attend Mount Allison University for further studies while also serving another church.

I did not spend enough time in Silver Falls to see a new sanctuary built during my short ministry, but it was gratifying to see that the Lord had blessed my ministry with many new worshipers, and the session was now convinced that a new building was needed. Before I left the congregation they had established a sizable building fund, and it was less than three years later that our family returned to the dedication ceremony of the new church.

(Please see photo of commemorative plaque in this book). Adding to the deep joy of the service was the baptism of our two children by a very dear friend, the Reverend Hugh John Flemming. It was a day of great blessing and an enormous encouragement for my future ministry.

Another type of new church development is starting an entirely new congregation. In a major denomination this usually requires an initiative that comes from a central church authority which in this case was the Presbytery of Cincinnati. Like most denominations they had a committee that was responsible for new church development. And so it was that one day, amidst my busy studies and work as a pastor, I had a call from the Presbytery with a proposal to start a new church in the nearby community of Delhi Hills, a suburb of Cincinnati. Accepting this new challenge would mean adding another year to my graduate studies, but despite my initial hesitation I felt God's call to begin such a challenging venture.

I began by renting the social hall in the Delhi Hills shopping center which was located more or less in the center of the suburb. Then we published a notice in the local newspaper that a new church under the name of "St. Paul's Presbyterian Church" was to be launched the following Sunday. After my wife and I arrived at the location shortly before 9:00 that morning (the service would run from 9:00 to 10:00 am to allow time for us to return to our church in Delhi and conduct the 11:00 am service) we discovered that a lectern, two chairs and a piano had been placed in the corner of the hall, along with two rows of folding chairs for the visitors. To add to the dubiously festive atmosphere a revolving sign above the lectern read "Drink Budweiser" in multi-colors! Just before the service began a "multitude" of three people arrived, a father with his two sons. After welcoming the visitors and a short prayer, my wife played the piano and we sang a few verses from a hymn printed on hand-outs. I preached a short sermon afterwards and reminded myself, despite my disappointment of such a small audience, of the Lord's promise that He will always be present even if only a few people meet in His Name.

The following Sunday a few more visitors attended the service and as time went on the empty chairs were filled with worshipers. Several months later we had to rent rooms in an elementary school across the street. We now had around 50 people and started Sunday school classes. After a year the little church grew to about 100 people – not fast enough for the Presbytery, though. Also, they lost interest in the project when I announced that I was leaving the area because I had graduated from the university and was headed for a college teaching job in Tennessee. But rather than closing the church in the absence of future Presbytery support, the newly elected church officers asked me to help them reorganize the small but highly motivated congregation into a non-denominational entity to be known as "The Bible Chapel of Delhi Hills." That was done with the Presbytery's consent, giving me the deep joy of leaving behind me a new evangelical witness for Christ as I heeded the Lord's call to serve Him in another area of Christian service.

Several years later when I was ministering in Colorado, I had a call from the Bible Chapel of Delhi Hills. They had built their own sanctuary and invited me to the dedication service. Unfortunately, I had other urgent appointments and was unable to attend the service. But I had the blessed assurance in my heart that, from a feeble beginning – a first sermon preached under a colorful rotating light inviting people to drink beer - there was now a new church preaching the Word of salvation to men, women and children. Most of them I never knew, but every one of them was dear to the heart of God. What a thrill to be used by God for building His kingdom!

But this was not the last time I found myself involved in church extension. During a very busy and happy life in the San Luis Valley I had found some time, among numerous other preaching assignments and lectures that took me across the United States and even Canada, to serve as guest teacher at two Bible Conference Centers of the International Torchbearer movement, an evangelistic organization. One of them was located north of San Antonio, Texas, and the other was in Estes Park, Colorado, a good three hour drive from my home in Del Norte. As is customary, these lectures were always open to the public and as a result I met quite a few people from the surrounding communities. In 1981 a group of ministers and business leaders got together and sponsored a panel discussion of the well-known book by Dr. Francis Schaeffer entitled "How Should we than Live?" (Crossway Books, 1983). As one of the foremost Christian thinkers of the twentieth century, the book contains an analysis and explanation for the decline of Western civilization in step with the erosion of Christian faith and morals. He argues that only a return to the Christian ethic, the acceptance of God's revelation in Scripture, and a new affirmation of Judeo-Christian morals would arrest the decline and, in time, prevent total collapse. The meeting drew a large crowd. I had been asked to chair the panel and their heated discussions and controversial conclusions made a profound impact on those who attended. And so I became somewhat known in the community of Estes Park, a scenic mountain town and gateway to the Rocky Mountain National Park, drawing about 3 million visitors every summer.

Several months after the meeting about Schaeffer's book, I had a call from a deacon of the First Baptist Church of Estes Park asking me a startling question: Would I consider a call to that church with the special task of building a new sanctuary for them? This sounded like a mighty challenge. Although the town had a permanent population of less than 6,000 year-round inhabitants at the time, Estes Park was a prominent tourist town year-round and peaked in the summer with large crowds of visitors and tourists coming from all over the world. It was indeed a strategic place for preaching the Word of God.

I thanked the deacon for his call and indicated that I needed some time to think and pray about his proposal. I was, of course, surprised and also thankful for this opportunity, and it came at a time when there were signs that my ministry in Del Norte, blessed as it was, was nearing completion and I was getting ready for a new challenge. And so, after many restless nights and fervent prayers for the Lord's guidance, I woke up one morning and felt ready to give the folk in Estes Park an affirmative answer for a personal visit and meeting with the church officers to discuss their proposal.

Several weeks later we gave a tearful farewell to our dear friends in Del Norte and moved to Estes Park. I had a strong feeling from the beginning that God had a special purpose for me in that church, and that our stay there would be relatively short. My main task was to help the congregation in the task of building a new sanctuary for the overflowing summer crowds and after that return to my own denomination.

The congregation, numbering about 300 regular members plus numerous year-round adherents was actually meeting in what had been two large buildings that had been joined together. Even two services in the morning and one in the evening could not accommodate the worshipers, especially during the peak tourist season. Plans and discussions for a new building had been carried on for several years but without results. Then somebody had brought up my name, which most of the church officers recognized from my teaching activities at the Torchbearer Center and the symposium for Dr. Schaeffer's book. Just how this Board agreed to consider me as their pastor I'll never know, but in retrospect it was one of the Lord's miracles in my life.

With the steady encouragement from the pulpit for increasing the already existing building fund it took about a year before we hired an architect and a contractor. The initial project called for more than a million dollar investment for a large sanctuary complete with meetings halls, offices and a sizeable gymnasium for recreation. The front of the building would face the famous icon of Estes Park, Long's Peak, at 14,255 feet the highest mountain in the National Park, looming majestically in the distance.

Building a new church requires a strong sense of purpose, unity and resolve. Prior to my accepting this new project I had been apprised by a friend from that community that I might face some problems in that regard. But I ignored the experience of others and forged ahead in the firm belief that if the Lord wanted me to help with the construction of a new sanctuary it was going to happen regardless of any obstacles. I don't believe that a church has ever been built without a variety of opinions within the congregation about its location, size, shape, and even the color of the carpet because that is human nature. The important task for me was to patiently reconcile all of these elements and with dedication and prayerful determination to proceed with the challenge.

While the building process was not without some problems, the new church emerged on the mountainside after about a year and the people gathered in praise of the Lord for giving them a new, spacious and beautiful place to worship. However, as I had anticipated, after the building was completed my mission was finished. I received a call to another church and saw it as a clear indication that my work in Estes Park after less than three years was done. The new, beautiful building was ready for use and dedicated just before I left. I felt that the essential purpose of my call, which had been to provide the extra leadership for the church officers, the congregation and the building committee, was fulfilled.

The Lessons Learned: There are arguably few areas of "success" in a pastor's ministry that enhance his reputation more than starting a new congregation or building a new sanctuary. They are often the result of a fruitful ministry. But we must always and humbly bear in mind the Apostle Paul's reminder: "I planted the seed, Apollos watered it, but God made it grow," (I. Cor. 3:6 NIV).

CHAPTER FOURTEEN

Disaster at Home

While teaching a Medieval History course at Covenant College I called upon a Catholic monk from a monastery in Atlanta, Georgia, to illuminate certain areas concerning the function of the Roman Catholic Church. I had discovered that monks are often excellent scholars whose penetrating insights into theology and church history can provide a superb learning experience. Over the years I got to know this saintly man quite well and one day we discussed the problems of being a pastor or priest. "There are too many distractions when the pastor has to worry about a wife and family," the monk offered, "I could never mix these roles and still be a faithful servant of God. I could not deal with the priorities of my ministry, not in terms of time or emotion."

It was not difficult to see his point, although one might argue that celibacy poses other problems that are mostly resolved in a marriage. Yet, it is true that the married pastor has to learn what exactly his priorities are to his wife and family and separate them from his duties to the congregation. There is no clear answer to that because every situation is different, but the call to being careful and vigilant of the dangers posed by too many commitments and, worse, too many distractions, are terribly real. I have often asked myself the question "did I spend enough time with my six children while they were growing up?" It is cold comfort to know that most fathers don't, and that the many reasons given for that failure can be quite ingenious sometimes revealing a lack of a sense of priority: "My work in the church produces constant stress and I need time for myself, like playing golf." That may be a legitimate activity but it better not encroach upon time spent with the family.

Most pastors learn to set up a workable balance dividing their time between family and work, but it usually means some compromise in time and commitment. There are those who claim, correctly, that the family comes first but what exactly does that mean? The reality is that married pastors with children minister to two "congregations," his natural and his church family. It is not difficult to understand that there exists a tension between the two as family needs can sometimes be overwhelming and take priority over everything else. That happens when tragedy strikes in the family which will place an extra heavy burden on the pastor as shown by the experience reported below. In any case, pastors are not exempt from sorrow and human failings. They must maintain constant vigil over their thoughts, faith and readiness to handle difficult situations and tragedies like anyone else, with the added burden that, unlike the people in their church, they may not have a pastor or other figure of spiritual authority looking out for them.

It was very early on a New Year's morning 1980 when the telephone rang in a home in Santa Paula, California, where our family was vacationing for the New Year's holidays. It was my oldest son, and he had very sad news: His wife had lost their first-born baby girl, Christian-Anne, the night before, on December 31st, to a condition known as "*placenta previa.*" God had taken the soul of the precious little child into the shining light of Heaven before she saw the dim light of day on earth.

Two hours later we were packed and ready to start the long drive home to Colorado, one of the saddest trips of my life. Then, while racing through the open Navajo Indian Reservation in Arizona, we were stopped by the native Indian police for speeding. A sympathetic officer let us go when I explained the reason for our haste, with the cautionary advice "to slow down so there won't be another death."

When we finally arrived in Del Norte it felt as if a black veil had been placed over the little town. People were close enough to each other that they shared their pain more intensely than in larger communities. My son had asked me to conduct the funeral for little Christian Anne, our first grand-daughter now lying in a little casket that looked out of place in the world of the living. People came from far and wide for the funeral service which I performed in a transfixed state of grief. A few people followed us to the cemetery on the bitterly cold morning where I was barely able to utter the words of the traditional ceremony adapted for children before I collapsed into the arms of a friend. How does a pastor bury his own grand child? In an agony of sorrow that can only be controlled by the Lord Himself Who "knows all our sorrows," and followed by an emotional shutdown that can only be appreciated by others who have had a similar experience. Yes, the tears in the desert flowed freely even as I realized God's mighty comfort through a veil of tearful eyes.

The immense sadness that results from the loss of a baby, however, is somewhat mitigated when we study the Word of God and find some reassuring passages of comfort. First, we learn that children are born in sin and that sin will control their lives until they repent and accept Christ as their Savior. Further, those who are too young to believe because they have not yet reached the age of accountability (being able to think for themselves and reason) are redeemed by the death of Christ and taken into heaven. Finally, our Lord Jesus Himself gave us these comforting words when He said this about children: "See that you do not look down on one of these little ones, for I will tell you that their angels in heaven always see the face of my Father in heaven," (Matth.18:10 NIV).

If disease, divorce and death are rated among the worst traumas that can happen in a person's life, I can testify to all of them. Little did I ever anticipate a shattering event in my life that would shake me to the foundations of my being, but I am relating it here as a warning to any pastor or Christian worker who thinks they are immune to personal disaster. After leaving a fruitful ministry in Lamar, Colorado, I left the pastorate temporarily and responded to the challenge of starting a Health Maintenance Organization (HMO) in Colorado Springs. I also taught several history courses at the local campus of the University of Colorado. Continuing my itinerant preaching career, all of these activities were enjoyable and rewarding, as were subsequent executive positions in the health care field in Oregon and California.

While developing the Qual-Med Health Maintenance Organization (HMO) in Colorado Springs at the invitation of a close friend who was CEO of the company, I became aware that my wife had suffered disenchantment with our marriage of thirty-three years. During a confrontation that followed she told me that I had nothing to worry about. Some time had passed and, after coming home from work one day, I was informed by our youngest and very distressed teenaged daughter that her Mum had left for England and shown no indication that she would return home.

My first reaction was shock and disbelief, soon followed by a sense of devastating loss as I was searching for a reasonable explanation for what had happened. Nothing, even the earlier warning signs of trouble, could have prepared me for this domestic disaster. I had learned from watching other couples going through the stages of divorce that it is unwise to start looking for blame. Marriage, like any other relationship, has many facets involving the whole gamut of human behavior, good and bad, but I faced a common problem I had seen before and now experienced with confusion and immense sadness: Not just that a radical separation had occurred, not just *what* had been done and what might have been corrected, but *how* it was done. I firmly believe that as Christians, regardless of the nature and magnitude of the problem, we must honestly discuss our differences and face them with earnest prayer for divine intervention and a possible solution, and not try to solve them by running away from them. In Christ there is always hope for reconciliation and one should never hurriedly abandon a long-term relationship regardless of the reasons. Whatever problems there were in our marital union of many years, I believed it had been by and large a caring relationship that had produced six wonderful children.

Many years later I was talking with my German friend Dean (aka Juergen) who is mentioned in the Sylt ammunition story told below. He was now living in Vancouver and we hadn't been in contact for some time. When I told him about my divorce he chuckled: "Karl, any woman who managed to live with you for more than thirty years is a saint." I had to agree, albeit somewhat reluctantly: A saint she was in the sense that our children could not have had a better mother. She raised them as a devoted Christian parent with a perfect mixture of deep affection and gentle discipline. After growing up, our two sons and four daughters were achievers in their own fields, models of law abiding citizens, free from vices and, in short, a family any Mum and Dad could be proud of.

One can learn many lessons from the experience of loss through separation and divorce. The most frequently mentioned, among many others, is the tendency of some pastors to become so involved in their work that they neglect their wife and family to the point that they miss signals of trouble in the relationship. With constant studies, challenging pastoral assignments and other tasks and distractions it is all too easy to change one's focus from marriage and family to the demands of the profession and other problems in life. However, there is never an excuse before God to put one's career, no matter how noble, before the welfare of one's family, even if it is due to compelling circumstances. God always has an answer to our problems whatever they are, but we often fail to listen and get carried away with our self-importance and ambition.

On the positive side I was recently reminded by one of my daughters that she has in her possession photos and color slides of our family taken at home, at picnics, special occasions, and long journeys that number in the thousands – most of them taken by me. That means that I spent perhaps more time with my family than I can remember and gives me some comfort. But it does little to lift the oppressive burden of feeling that I was less the good dad of six children and the noble husband of a wife who needed me when so often I was not there for them. In the final analysis I can only say that broken relationships are usually the cause of moral and spiritual failures for which only God has the solution. They are perhaps part of the failure God expects of us mentioned toward the end of this chapter and resolved by His mercy and grace. If we are sensitive to the working of His Spirit in our lives after the hardship and tears of contrition that are the inevitable consequences of our failures, then we can learn lessons of humility and dependence on Him that we rarely learn from anything else.

Another lesson I learned from this experience was that pastors cannot expect much sympathy and practical help from most of their associates and friends in times of crisis. Because people regard them as spiritually and morally "above" others when, in fact, they are not different from any forgiven sinner, there is a silent stigma attached to a pastor who fails, whether in the pulpit or in private relationships. But a close and compassionate friend assured me many times that God had what he called "an even better companion" for me in the future. It was hard to believe at the time but it turned out to be true.

To my great joy my youngest son was the best counsellor and comforter I had, apart from bringing my burden before the Lord, and for almost seven years I had to learn to live by myself after being surrounded by a dearly beloved wife and the affection of a large and wonderful family. Our youngest daughter had just graduated from high school and was ready to leave for college.

I wrote the preceding paragraphs with hesitation and a careful focus on the facts. If I ever had any malice or anger about all this, it has dissipated a long time ago. Unfortunately, I cannot say the same about my feelings of guilt, inadequacy, and failure in my calling as a pastor. Several years passed by before I preached again - in the Reformed Church of Denver - as I felt unworthy to serve my Lord in that capacity. The process of self-forgiveness took many more years. In some ways a person sensitized by the Holy Spirit never fully copes with a trauma like divorce. Some people say it's worse than death because any fragrant memories of love and devotion are forever tarnished if not completely destroyed, although time, the great healer, can and has mitigated that loss in my case. Yes, the pain of failure, separation and loneliness caused "the tears in the desert to flow." It brought to mind a conversation I had with my spiritual mentor Major Ian Thomas many years ago while we were driving to a meeting in Central England. The Major's question was: "Karl, tell me what exactly does God expect of you?" Brimming with confidence I responded: "Faith, trust and obedience!" He shook his head, "no." I tried another track: "Loyalty, service, humility." He shook his head again and left me stunned. After a pause the great English evangelist taught me a lesson with one word: "Failure!" The moral and theological implications of his answer are much too deep to discuss in this book. But we have one stunning example of failure recorded in the Gospels when Peter, after affirming his loyalty to Christ even until death (Luke 22:33 NIV) he fulfilled his Master's prediction that he would deny him three-times. The key lesson here is that sometimes God uses failure to bend human pride and demolish our autonomy so that later we may be able to serve Him with greater dedication and resolve. But the message was clear and reminded me of Jesus' words in Matthew 5:48 (NIV) where He challenges His audience with various aspects of their social and spiritual relationships ending with the words "be ye perfect, therefore, as your Heavenly Father is perfect." Clearly, a saved sinner can only be "made perfect" through Christ but the road to that state of superior being does not end on this side of eternity because no matter how hard we try, our walk with Him will be marked by our failures, as I have shown above. When I have concluded that **my work** for the Lord defines my faith rather than **my walk** with Him I become confused about my priorities, both as a Christian and as a pastor, and I am surely headed for the failure He expects of me. I am also forcefully reminded that all I am and all I do is by Him and through Him.

On the positive side, the experience has given me a better understanding and deeper empathy for those who have suffered similar distress and agony.

The Lessons Learned: The pastor is exposed to the same perils as his parishioners. Nobody is exempt from moral or spiritual failure, from physical tragedy, deadly errors and misunderstanding. The long list of "heroes of the faith" recorded for us in the history of the Old Testament are also of men who sometimes failed to obey God. It is only by the awareness of our full dependence on Him and constant vigil over our thoughts and deeds that we can resist the sins of the flesh. Failure is the norm, not the exception. But, as I have learned, it is failure that God expects and uses to discipline us for a closer walk with Him. He is the One Who, after all, can cause the wrath of man to praise Him and transform even our worst mistakes for His glorious purpose.

CHAPTER FIFTEEN

When it takes a Miracle

One should not be surprised that the God of all miracles as revealed to us in the Old and New Testaments is still performing acts and intervening in the lives of His servants that defy any rational explanation. Webster's Collegiate Dictionary defines a miracle as "an extraordinary event manifesting divine intervention in human affairs." The Bible is full of divine miracles recorded to us by the inspired writers of Scripture, but just a few examples from both the Old and the New Testaments will suffice for this chapter. By the way, I am placing this chapter toward the end of this book because miracles cover my whole life and in some way determine what and who we are from day to day.

In the Old Testament we find almost eighty miracles, including God's destruction of Sodom and Gomorrah (Gen. 19:24); ten plagues of Egypt (Ex.7:14-25) and the Diving of the Red Sea (Ex. 14: 21-31). In the New Testament our Lord Jesus Christ used miracles to authenticate His power as the Son of God. Among the many miracles He performed there is the healing of the two blind men (Matth.9:27-31), the feeding of 5000 people with only two loaves of bread and five fishes (Matth.14:13-21), and the raising of Lazarus from the dead (John 11:38-44).

But perhaps the greatest miracle of all is that God, in His mysterious love for sinful humanity, decided to save us by sacrificing His Own, sinless Son, to die for us that by His vicarious death we may be saved from our sin and forgiven for all eternity. I confess to God every day my total lack of understanding His love and that He gave Himself on the Cross to save a wretched sinner like me from eternal punishment.

With that in mind it is perhaps not so difficult to believe, if not to understand, the many miracles Jesus performed during His earthly ministry, and the endless stream of miracles God causes to happen in the lives of those who are "predestined to be saved." Miracles happen although we don't always know it. Most Christians I have known over the years have stories to tell that are incredible, but they are bona fide experiences sent from God, whether for healing, encouragement, intervention, or even physical escape from terminal illness or death.

Because this book is about my own life I shall confine my stories of miracles to just a few. But I hasten to add that whatever miracles I experienced in my life, they are vastly out-trumped by those of others, whether in Christian work, the military, on hospital beds, or in a multitude of other circumstances. In that light I'm not really sure how much the following stories of God's intervention in my life can contribute to this book other than to remind anyone contemplating Christian service that God will indeed use miracles if they are required to convince, equip, or protect one for His work of kingdom building.

I should also mention here that some of the stories can be found in my book, "From Hitler to Christ," (The Doug Glenn Company, 2013). But I feel that these little dramas of life tell a much bigger story – they are a vital part of my spiritual experience and produced their fair share of the deepest emotions of praise, wonder and contrition – in short, some very real but special "tears in the desert." I shall present each story with a brief caption for the reader's convenience.

I. A Knock on the Door

By the year 1936 the Nazis had fully consolidated their totalitarian power in Germany, and the search for people of Jewish ancestry living in the general population had begun. At the time the German people did not know the full extent of the atrocities the Nazi Government would commit, but it is doubtful even in those early days of racial persecution much could have been done to stop it.

The knock on the door was loud and authoritative. When my foster mother opened the door she was confronted by two men wearing grey overcoats and black hats. They introduced themselves as "government agents with official business." My foster mother knew instinctively that something was very wrong. I was told to go to my room while she and the two men talked in the living room. After a while one of the men entered my room and quite cheerfully began asking me questions. I was only five years old but, like most German youngsters, had a real crush on our beloved "Fuehrer." That seemed to please the visitor. And yes, I was looking forward to joining the Hitler Youth as soon as I was old enough, and absolutely with the encouragement of my foster parents. What activities did I enjoy most? I responded innocently but mischievously with a remark that I have remembered verbatim all my life: *"Oh, Ich fuehle mich sauwohl mit meiner Rasselbande,"* (I feel just great - like a pig wallowing in the mud - with my gang of miscreants.) I then proceeded boastfully giving the "nice man" a brief summary of our juvenile – and mildly delinquent – activities, most of them of the kind that annoyed our neighbors more than they harmed them. The stranger laughed out loud and we continued our happy conversation for several more minutes before the other man appeared in the room and asked to speak to his companion. They left the room and shortly afterwards returned with my foster mother. "Good to meet you, little fellow," the kind man said to me, *"Auf Wiedersehen."* After both men had left I noticed my foster mother shaking from head to toe and then breaking down in tears. She never told me why and refused to answer my questions, leaving me wondering why anyone could be so upset over such a nice visit.

Well, *"Auf Wiedersehen"* it was. Several weeks later we had a repeat visit from two "government agents." I do not recall if they were the same men. Their visit seemed shorter this time and they did not talk with me again. But their conversation with my foster mother, once over, had turned her into a nervous wreck shaking like a reed and sobbing so hard that she was unable to talk. No wonder – these men and the two of the previous visit were from the "Resettlement Office," an innocuous name for a division of the dreaded Gestapo (Secret State Police). Their task was to locate, identify, and sent all persons, regardless of age, classified as "racially impure" by the Nazi Government to one of its concentration or labor camps.

I knew nothing of my peril at the time and it was almost fifteen years later when my foster mother told me that I was a quarter Jewish. That meant by Nazi racial standards that I was a *"Mischling zweiten Grades"* (a person of both Aryan and Jewish or other "racially inferior" descent) and that the Gestapo had tracked me down. I have no doubt to this day that the Lord saved me from the deadly fate I would have suffered had I been arrested by these men. After failing to do so after two visits most people agree that I was saved by a miracle

2. A Parrot's Urgent Call

The danger of anti-aircraft fire was not confined to the crews and airplanes dropping bombs overhead but also to the intended victims below because the anti-aircraft shells disintegrated after exploding and their debris fell to the ground, posing a dangerous hazard to the population. It was therefore strongly advised to stay inside during air raids in order to avoid being hit by the shrapnel from these exploding shells, including pieces of sharp metal that could weigh up to a pound.

One day in the summer of 1944 I was standing in front of our cabin located in the countryside about thirty miles from our apartment in Hamburg watching an air raid in progress over the city. I heard the explosions of bombs some distance away but felt safe realizing that the bombers, judging by the anti-aircraft fire, were not directly overhead. But I had not taken into account that several batteries of anti-aircraft artillery were located not far from our cabin.

While enjoying the deadly show of the search lights getting the enemy airplanes into their crosshairs and rows of tracer ammunition followed by heavier artillery headed for them in the distance, I suddenly heard our Lora, the family parrot, shriek out loudly with a familiar phrase, "Oma, herkomm" (grandma, come here). There was no grandmother in our household but Lora, our beloved feathered pet, had obviously been taught that phrase during her transit from South America. She was a tall handsome bird adorned with green, yellow and red feathers. The stately pet had been brought to Germany by my foster father on a large steam ship from South America some years before the war. Her loud and repeated call *"Oma herkomm"* was bad German grammar but an urgent summons to go and see her. Lora usually enjoyed the noise of air raids and sometimes had the audacity of praising the attackers with her version of "God bless America," which sailors had also taught her on the ship during its long voyage. But now she seemed unusually agitated, continuing her passionate cry *"Oma, herkomm, Oma herkomm."* I wasn't grandma but her plea could apply to anyone and I felt that something was wrong. I turned around and took one step into the house to calm the bird when I heard a loud, metallic clinking noise behind me. The round bottom of an 88-mm anti-aircraft shell had smashed into the iron grill in front of the door and left a big dent in it exactly where I had been standing a split-second before. Deeply moved I went over to the bird who was now quite calm again, picked her up and held her close to my chest. Her response, as always, was "Koepfen kraulen" (cuddle my little head). Lora had more than earned it. She had miraculously saved me from serious injury if not worse. Could one claim that it was divine providence?

3. More than Seashells

The Island of Sylt off the coast of the North German Province of Schleswig Holstein near the border of Denmark is located in the turbulent North Sea, just a few miles offshore of the Province of Schleswig Holstein. Before the war it was connected to the mainland by a railroad dam which added to its access and popularity as a choice tourist destination known for its beautiful beaches stretching along the west coast, and sand dunes of gleaming white sand when the sun rose high.

While largely an island paradise for the rich and independent, visitors preferred staying near its only town, Westerland. Our school group occupied a famous youth camp known as "Klappholtztal" about 5 miles North of Westerland and within a few minutes' walk to "Little Abyssinia" a quaint name for a nudist colony we were discouraged from visiting. The rest of the island was deserted, most of the beaches covered with debris from sunken ships that had floated ashore during the war and never been recovered. After the restrictive war years with their many deprivations, including hardly any travel, a week at the youth camp sponsored by our high school was welcomed with much enthusiasm and eager anticipation.

The adventure began with a boisterous bus ride from Hamburg to Sylt, and the excitement of seeing the ocean knew no end. The accommodations were simple, if not Spartan. This was the late summer of 1946. It had been just over a year and a half since the war ended, but the shortages of food and almost all other consumer goods were still widespread, especially in the big cities. So it was a welcome surprise to find some fresh fruit and vegetables on the island which were unavailable back home.

Lying in the sun or playing various ball games on the beach were entertaining activities, but for my friend Juergen (after his immigration to Canada known as "Dean") and I soon became boring, causing us to look for other adventures that had more "fun." Walking north along the beach for miles, we began to look for seashells and the famous "sea stars" which, once dried out properly, could be sold back home as ornaments or decorations. But we also noticed that the ocean was washing ashore a lot of seemingly useless debris. But then we noticed a black metal box measuring about fifteen inches all the way round. Salt water had made the writing illegible, but after prying the tight lid open with my ever handy pocket knife we found that it contained pure cocoa. Most of it was still usable and we shared our find with the other students back at the camp.

Our curiosity in what we came across on the beach and detected floating in the surf grew by the day, and soon we did our best to drag various items onto the beach. Most of them were useless parts of ship wreckage and things thrown overboard, but one day we spotted two mysterious metal boxes being pushed ashore by the surf. Drab green in color they measured about three feet long and eighteen inches square. After prying the clamps open on the first box we stared at sixteen 37mm ammunition shells inside, all in like-new condition. We buried both boxes in a sand dune and returned to the site the following day and, sure enough, another box was trying to make it ashore.

But there was a problem with this treasure: What could we possibly do with all this ammunition? There were strict laws against Germans owning any kind of ordnance, and we knew that the mere possession of our new treasure could get us into deep trouble. We most certainly could not take even one of these shells back to Hamburg without being detected. The logical conclusion was to try and salvage some of the parts inside our deadly find and have fun with them later. Lacking any tools to separate the warhead from the brass shell, we "ingeniously" solved the problem by smashing the ordnance over the edge of one of the steel plates locally known as "Buehnen." They were buried in the sand vertically and extended far out to the water to help prevent beach erosion. Conveniently for us, they had 2-inch holes on top enabling us to stick the projectile into a hole and then jumping on the brass shell until it broke loose from it. Most people would agree that this was an extremely crude method – "a dance of death" - second only in danger to smashing the shell over the metal edge, but it proved to be very effective. My friend and I had now formed a partnership for disarming live ammunition, and saving the various components for a purpose as yet undetermined. The terms "black market trade" and "fireworks" did come to mind.

From the beginning of our new hobby we had one concern: What type of fuse did these shells have? Was it an impact fuse without or with a delayed timer, or did it have a set timer, as most anti-aircraft shells did. Then, after opening up a few shells we noticed that the tip of the shell – the timer – had come apart and what we were looking at was a thick, aluminum-colored pin pointing directly at the little cylinder of Amatol or Nitro-Glycerin which had the power to explode the warhead. Jurgen and I agreed that after this discovery we had to be "more careful."

For the next week my friend and I left the camp early and headed for the beach right after breakfast. After dragging several more boxes from the surf we "processed" shell after shell and laboriously separated the parts onto blankets: the propellant bags containing black powder shaped like chocolate raisins, and the long "spaghetti" sticks of gun powder that filled the brass shell. Next we had to deal with the projectile or warhead. After unscrewing the small aluminum cone, the timer, from the top, we removed the base plug packed with an explosive the size of a roll of film designed to help the projectile stay on course after it separated from the brass. Then came the most delicate part of all: Extracting the small cylindrical capsule of Amatol or nitro-glycerin from the projectile. Tightly sealed and measuring no more than 2 cm x .4 cm with the power to blow the warhead apart upon impact, it was seated right in front of the needle. We correctly identified this part as the most "powerful" to be treated with extra caution!

As if disarming .37mm ammunition was not reckless enough, two days before our trip back to Hamburg, Jurgen and I discovered a sea mine that had been washed against the sand dunes by the tide. The protruding metal tubes that contained the detonators, technically called "Hertz Hornes," had been bent, and my friend decided that he was going to "straighten them out" by pounding them upright with a heavy rock. But before he could strike the first blow a pole-vaulting couple screamed at us from a distance, "Stop! Stop! Stop! Don't do that!" After they arrived they looked extremely upset and shouted at us "If you want to blow yourselves to hell, just wait until we are out of sight," quickly resuming their run along the beach. There followed a heated argument about the merits of the souvenir value of a mine detonator compared with our lives, but I finally convinced my determined friend that our lives were definately preferable to something we might never own anyway!

During the early afternoon of the same day the area was shaken by a loud explosion which shook our camp. We heard later that British commandos had blown up a live navy mine after receiving a report that two teenagers had tried to tamper with it. My friend and I eagerly agreed with the other students and our teacher that nobody could be that stupid and reckless!

The question remains: How could two teenaged boys be so reckless? In short, the reasons were a mixture of disillusionment with broken Nazi promises causing an indifference and almost fatalistic attitude toward life, a sense of boredom and curiosity, combined with the usual youthful desire for thrills and adventure. Then again, nobody is immune to insanity.

Before our return to Hamburg a few of our trusted friends joined us for a special "farewell party" during which we burned the large pile of explosive material – minus the nitro glycerin – and after an enormous fire that could be seen for miles we concluded our "vacation adventure" with feelings of great achievement ending in a proud celebration with a select group of fellow students we could trust.

For the return trip to Hamburg we had stuffed large quantities of explosive materials into our baggage and that of other students with their eager consent. After boarding the chartered bus on the mainland we narrowly escaped detection of the contraband during a search by the British Military Police.

But the story doesn't end there. Eager to be the first to "free" the nitroglycerin from its small cylindrical capsule (we had brought about two dozen of them back with us) it was my friend Jurgen who succeeded first – and blew three fingers of his left hand while at the same time demolishing the living room of his house. During my hospital visit he greeted me with a grin which belied that he was suffering acute pain: "Look at it this way, only three fingers. It could have been worse." Indeed, the odds of survival while smashing several dozen 37 mm ammunition shells on steel plates to crack them open for their contents were obviously very small, but then nobody I know has ever been foolish enough to try it. In retrospect from a Christian point of view I like to think the whole episode was a miracle of divine protection, a feat of survival against very high odds, one that fits somehow into the pattern of my life.

Finally, the problem of heavy pollution of the North and Baltic seas by military ordnance is an ongoing problem to this day. In an article entitled "German Waters Teeming with World War II Munitions," the German news magazine "Der Spiegel on Line," (April 11, 2013) Carsten Holm writes, "More than fifty million bombs, mines, shells, detonators and cartridges from World War II are rusting on the ocean floor of the North and Baltic Seas or are *washed up on beaches*" (emphasis my own). Authorities are opting not to remove the ordnance – and hoping that no one gets hurt." Unfortunately, at least one guy already did.

4. Trusting God to Provide

It would take many more pages to relate all of God's miracles in my life, but I shall close this chapter with a few of the most amazing marvels of God's provision in my life. This theme has been a part of my Christian life to this day, but a few highlights will demonstrate God's faithfulness and the argument that "God never calls a man to serve Him without preparing and equipping him first."

(a) Theology and Missions in Scotland

The entry in my passport was short and clear: "Student, not allowed to work paid or unpaid." Here I am referring to my previously mentioned studies in Scotland, but this time in the context of what I consider a miracle of divine provision because I had no idea how I going to pay for them. After the tall and kindly man by the name of Geoffrey Grogan, the Dean of Students, studied my application and passport he looked at me and smiled: "I assume that you still have no money to put down with your application?" "No Sir, I'm sorry." Another smile, this time reassuring, "Don't worry, if the Lord has called you, he will provide." Prophetic words indeed.

As referred to earlier, I was half-way through my courses when I was told almost casually, during a visit to the Christian Conference in England, that "all of my college expenses, tuition and board, had been paid." Paid by whom? By a former British army officer I hardly knew. He was wounded in battle against the Germans and had hated them ever since. God spoke to the retired colonel and after he became a Christian gave him a love for the lost German youths. During a totally unexpected and unplanned trip with this man and two other students from Scotland to the Southern British coast I had a fifteen-minute conversation with him while we were walking along the beach. After our return to Scotland I never saw him again. Who can ever doubt God's provision when we trust Him?

(b) From the Shetland Islands to Canada

This story begins with my call to study for the ministry in Canada, raising the immediate question how I was going to raise the required funds for an expensive trans-Atlantic steamship passage for two adults and a little baby boy. I had shared our new opportunity with a few friends and asked them to pray with us for God's provision as a sure sign that He wanted us to go to the New World.

After several weeks, as the time for our proposed departure was near, I received a letter from Detroit, Michigan. It was from a German couple, Anna and Leonard Rahnhofer, who had immigrated to the U.S. some time prior to World War II. Anna wrote that she had heard of my opportunity to go to Canada and told me that they had never forgotten what I had done for their adopted son, Bernard, a young boy in Hamburg. He had lost his parents and sister during one of the air raids over Hamburg and, although several years younger than I, I had befriended him and taught him English after he was invited to move to the U.S. for adoption by the Rahnhofers. Now, she declared, it was their turn to help me. How much money did we need for the travel expense from the Shetland Islands via England to travel to Saint John, New Brunswick?

I was deeply moved and realized that so often when we help others without selfish motives God "rewards" us for our generosity, sometimes many years later and well above of what we deserve. After moving to North America I had the opportunity to finally get to know the Rahnhofers face to face while visiting their lovely home in Detroit, and what an affectionate encounter it was!

(c) *No Place to Go*

After completing my graduate studies at the University of Pennsylvania in May, 1961, we returned to Canada for my theological education at the Atlantic School of Theology in Halifax, Nova Scotia. But there was a problem: With a wife and three small children we had no income and no place to live. The Department of Home Missions was looking for a student pastorate I would serve during my studies – as I had before in New Brunswick – but there were no openings.

Most graciously the seminary opened its doors for us and we were comfortably settled in one of the small dormitories with use of the kitchen. However, these arrangements were made under the condition that we had to move out by August 1, when the first resident students were expected to arrive and some classes scheduled to begin.

June, July and most of August passed and we had no place to go. By the end of August we had packed all of our belongings ready to move on – but where? It was now August 29th and almost 10:00 in the evening, a beautiful and quiet day. Standing outside the main entrance of the college with a friend and enjoying the brisk air we saw a car driving up. My heart thumped as I recognized the visitor as the Reverend Dr. Bill Godfrey, Superintendent of Missions for our Conference. He greeted me with an open smile shaking my hand vigorously: "Good news, Karl. The church in Newport has agreed to extend a call to you as a student minister. They want you to start immediately." Tears of gratitude and joy flowed from my face. Indeed, our Heavenly Father always enables us for the task to which He calls us. Before I complete this exciting adventure of God's unfailing provision, I will say this: Nothing characterizes my life more than God's protection and provision.

(d) No End to God's Blessings

Like so many other Christian workers, including retired pastors, after my retirement from the pastorate I found myself with limited financial resources. I kept active pursuing a variety of tasks, including some preaching and teaching, and for a few years prior to the recession of 2008 helped my youngest son, who was always most generous with me, in his consulting business. But the economic recession of 2008 hit us very hard. It effectively wiped out our 401(k) business retirement plan and jeopardized a significant investment in a Canadian mining project. In short, whatever savings and investments we had accumulated over the years were almost gone overnight, and the prospects for a comfortable retirement looked grim – from the human point of view.

At this point in my life I had only my wife and myself to support, but our income, while average for most retired Americans my age, was marginal when considering our monthly expenses, especially payments for housing and a gradually accumulated debt. I was somewhat concerned but strangely never worried about all this, knowing from my personal experience of God's provision that there was no time limit to His faithfulness.

After the recession of 2009 started my son secured a well-paying executive job with a national company, causing me to consider another mission as I did not want to be a burden to his failing business. I had always been touched by my brother-in-law Simon's work as a lay missionary in the hinterland of Colombia and offered to help by organizing a tax exempt Christian mission to help finance his growing expenses. At the same time I was also considering helping him on the mission field on a part-time basis without actually moving back to Colombia. It seemed therefore a good idea to move from Colorado to Florida because Bogota is only a three-hour flight from Miami. Further, another brother-in-law owned a condo in Naples which we were able to occupy for a reasonable rent payment. After setting up "Itinerant Ministries Colombia" (IMC) my wife and I made a trip to her country to help set up things on the ground. However, when we got there we were informed that Simon, unable to support his ministry any longer from the sale of Christian books and Bibles, had taken a business job and reduced his itinerant ministry to weekends. Clearly, God had closed the door. But this fact did nothing to dispel my deep conviction that He had sent us to Florida for a purpose.

Several years passed before that purpose became clear. My wife and I had attended a small Evangelical Church in our neighborhood which was to become a fountainhead of divine blessings. It wasn't long before the pastor asked me to preach for him when he was out of town. As always, we met some of the dearest people and knew that we had found our church home.

When my brother-in-law decided to sell his condo we helped him find a buyer and, before we had started even looking for another place to live, an elder in the church offered us his second house on his beautiful estate which was vacant at the time. About two years later, after the elder's wife passed away and he made plans to sell his estate, the Lord answered our prayers for a new home in a very dramatic way. He also blessed us with new friends in a way we had never experienced before, although over my many years of ministry I had met some truly wonderful people and made relationships with some in the bonds of faith that endure to this day.

One of them happened following a church service one Sunday morning when a very dignified gentleman, accompanied by his elegant wife, engaged me in a conversation. As we became better acquainted I was increasingly amazed about our unity of thought about the Bible, Christian doctrines, and their application to the realities of life. I felt that I found a true "alter ego." Little did we know at the time that God was going to bless us through this dedicated Christian couple in ways that could only be described as truly "miraculous."

Over a short period of time the Lord's loving providence helped us cover a string of unexpected expenses, beginning with my daughter Annette's death in August, 2012. When it looked like we needed to replace our aging car, God gave us a new car. When we were looking for a new place to live and worried about the rent or lease, God gave us a house – without a mortgage! And when, partly due to helping family members in need, we were facing a serious amount of unpaid financial obligations, God gave us the money to pay off all our debts. Today, at the sunset of my life, I can sing a prayer of thanksgiving to the Lord for His faithfulness. We may not be rich in the material sense, but we own everything we have. The "Tears in the Desert" are no longer shed in a lonely pastor's study, but during our daily devotions in our living room as we celebrate our Lord's bountiful protective and providential care in keeping with His promises. They are, indeed, more often the tranquil tears of joy.

The Lessons Learned: Few other things in life than the miracles wrought by God bring a more vivid awareness and strengthen a believer's faith in His Being and love. What is surprising to me is that the experience of a miracle is sometimes pushed into the background of my memory, and I am surprised when I see God's hand at work again – and again. I have come to realize that all pastors experience miracles in their ministry, dramatic divine interventions of different types depending on the situation, to demonstrate His nearness and caring for his often perplexed servants. Why are we so reluctant to acknowledge what God is doing in our lives?

I am reminded of a passage recorded about the ministry of Jesus where He asserts His deity and asks the Jews who wanted to stone Him to "believe the miracles" as confirmation that He is, indeed, the Son of God (John 10:37-38; see also 14:11 NIV). But even His miracles were not enough to convince His enemies and, alas, so many times not even His followers, including myself, fail to give Him the full credit for the miraculous events in our lives. And yet, when I remember God's hand intervening in my life, my mind tells me that the event was far beyond "coincidence" and I cry out to God in praise and thanksgiving. Expect miracles in the ministry, miracles of protection, miracles of provision, miracles of preservation and even survival. It will give you confidence in Him like nothing else and make your labors for Him more effective, and finally fill your eyes with the tears of joy.

CHAPTER SIXTEEN

Retirement but not Retreat!

Because I served only one more pastorate after my retirement, the following is a summary of the many lessons I learned in retirement in addition to those the Lord taught me over many years of service for Him. Perhaps the most important one is that pastors would do well to prepare for this time as it has its own stressors or obligations that may not have been considered during a busy life of ministry. But these years are an important part of my life and serve to bring home the reality of God's providence as nothing else. Lessons are also learned in the sunset years of life when one's vision goes dim, one's step becomes less sure, and one's sense of eternity becomes ever more real.

My official retirement from the United Presbyterian Church (USA) came on June 1, 1996, thirty-two years after I was received by the Presbytery of Cincinnati, and three days after my 65th birthday. As already discussed I had chosen a tent-making ministry for some time, combining occasional preaching and teaching with a demanding career in the health care field (HMO and PPO). Two years before, during a trip to South America, I met the new love of my life, Sofia, an intelligent and beautiful young woman from Colombia. She brought a lovely little five-year old girl into our marriage and my happiness was complete. We settled in Southern California and while living in Costa Mesa and Tustin I also taught at the University of California (Irvine), a good position for meeting many interesting people and a fertile field for Christian witness.

In 1998, through a recommendation from a business friend, I was invited by the owners of a company that manufactured medical equipment in Mexico to join their executive staff for an evaluation and updating of their production processes and international marketing systems. Their mainline products were medical implants and surgical instruments, some of them imported from Germany. My wife, daughter and I arrived in the City of Puebla (about 90 miles from Mexico City) in early April. We rented a specious home on a mountain side with a full view of two famous volcanos, enrolled our daughter in school, and got busy in the company.

My official position was that of "special advisor to the Chairman and CEO," and my task was daunting but also fascinating as we worked to bring the company up to modern production and marketing techniques, addressed personnel issues like improved medical coverage for the workers, a profit sharing system and more vacation time. We also expanded our overseas marketing operations in Germany and Switzerland and started a new import program from Pakistan. Apart from an extended trip to Europe I also travelled once a week to our Sales office in Mexico City in order to help expand the company's lucrative business with the Mexican Government, and once attended an orthopedic trade show in Acapulco. After three very busy years I felt that my goals for the company had been fulfilled and, although urged to stay on, we moved to the small expatriate town of Ajijic on scenic Lake Chapala near Guadalajara. There we bought and for several months operated a furniture store with a fully staffed sewing center. We decided to sell the business in 2002 and moved to Colombia, my wife's exotic home country. Sightseeing and exploring the stunning landscapes of that country, including mountains soaring to 20,000 feet, and enjoying the tropical beaches of the Caribbean, was a pastime I could have gotten used to.

In 2005 we returned to Colorado to help my youngest son in his growing consulting business, with the intention of staying no longer than a year. But God had other plans for us and we spent four years in Boulder and Longmont before moving to Florida for our final retirement. Prior to that I had accepted the advice of my youngest son and wrote a book about my long and convoluted spiritual journey, covering my years in Nazi Germany all the way to my conversion in England. As mentioned earlier, my preaching career continued in the Sunshine State where we finally made our permanent home.

Most people understand that men who enter the pastorate are not expecting financial rewards. This is not just a "job" that provides financial security, although God's providence is always at work to meet every legitimate need, and when one faces difficult situations, miracles can and will happen, as they did in our lives. This is a story the details of which would make another book, but in the context of what I learned during many years in the pastorate, one can absolutely rely on the Lord's guidance and provision every step of the way. I can testify to it with grateful enthusiasm as a minister living with limited financial resources almost all of my professional life, but supporting a wife and six children without major financial problems and later my second family including another precious little daughter. I also recall with greatest satisfaction that God rewarded us all with excellent health as we raised our children. Indeed, the Lord's blessings come to us in many different ways even if one earns only a modest monthly salary.

Retirement is, of course, not without troubles and even tragedies. My daughter Annette who had served as a field reporter and later as a news-anchor for a television station in Colorado Springs, developed a series of illnesses over several years caused by a breakdown of her immune system. Whether it was due to taking large doses of various allergy medications in her younger years compounded by other factors we shall never know. But it was with increasing concern that our whole family watched her getting steadily worse. Finally, in early August of 2012, our precious daughter passed away at the young age of 49, leaving behind two teen-aged children and a family in shock and tears. They say it is unnatural for a child to die before her parents, but God is merciful and brings comfort amidst the most trying events of life. It is now more than five years later and there is hardly a day that I do not think about her. It seems that those called of God to serve Him must bear their own private sorrow on top of mourning for the congregations they serve, and that the solemnity of passing from this world to the next is a continues reminder of our most important work as

"Seelsorgers:" To help save souls from perdition and prepare them lovingly for their passage to heaven.

Finally, it is with the tears of joyous gratitude that we thank God every day for the caring Christian brothers and sisters in our life who have so generously contributed to our material and spiritual welfare, but even beyond that shared their Christian love and lives with us so that we could also enjoy the privilege of their friendship.

The Lessons Learned: Retirement from a busy life in the pastorate and involvement in many other activities offers a time of rest, relaxation and reflection, but it also brings its own stress. Pastors do well to prepare carefully for this time in their sunset years as they face a life with less strength and more illness, often with financial resources insufficient to meet all of their needs, and the widespread indifference toward old people that is an unfortunate feature of our society. But in contrast to the popular notion, God is never finished with his servants until He calls them home. The "tears in the desert" continue to flow in different directions, but those shed in sorrow are also mixed with joy and praise for His abundant goodness in the faith that binds us to His eternal purpose. After His initial call God never lets His servant go. He must always expect an assignment to yet another task until His final call to his heavenly home, and there he will only shed the tears of eternal peace and joy!

CONCLUSION

Even the most ambitious and ingenious effort of writing the story of my Christian ministry extending over half a century is limited by my memory, my ability to select the most appropriate examples to demonstrate my arguments, and my lack of focus on the unseen powers behind the human activities I have described and tried to explain here.

As stated in the beginning of this book, this is not an attempt to analyze the numerous and complex components that define the ministry, but simply an effort to give a snapshot of my career as a pastor including the major lessons I learned from it. Therefore, I am concluding my story with a summary of some additional advice drawn from these lessons in the form of what I believe to be the personal qualities desirable for a successful ministry. They focus on what a person ***is*** rather than what a person ***does*** and the enumerations of personal advice begin with an exhortation of striving ***"to be"*** so that when God calls us to serve Him, we can labor toward a fruitful work of kingdom building. But the Lord also encourages us, as a father does his children, to cry out to Him for help so that we will not be alone as we shed the tears of joy or sorrow in the desert. Following is my advice:

Be Yourself. The pulpit is not a stage. The preacher is not actor, and the people in the pew will realize very soon when you are not authentic but try and be somebody else.

Be Faithful to His Word. Don't turn Biblical preaching and teaching into lectures that have little or no spiritual meaning and would be more appropriate in a secular or academic setting.

Be Disciplined. Learn to manage your time, your money and all of your other resources. Be punctual for all appointments and diligent in your work. Give your energy to the Lord never compromising any activity for Him. Always do what you say you will do.

Be Compassionate. Weep with those who weep, let your heart shape your words of comfort and encouragement, and learn to lift up those who are down with the strength Christ gives you in times of need.

Be Available. A man or woman of God is never too busy not to respond to urgent needs that come up suddenly. Learn to be there when people need you, and when time is of the essence.

Be Open-Minded. Exhibiting an open mind and heart to people in trouble does not mean that you condone their conduct or approve unconfessed sin, but it opens the door to communication and prayer.

Be Versatile. Nobody can be all things to all people, but one can try and discover hidden talents never used before. It is better to fail in something than never trying to meet a challenge.

Be Honest and Ethical. Pastors, as pointed out above, are not paragons of moral virtue, but they must set an example for other Christians even if they risk moral failure. They must strive for virtue even if they are, like any other Christian, forgiven sinners.

Be Generous. Tithe if you can and be open-handed with your time and talent. Your moral conscience includes your responsibility to all people in need, even if your practical ability to help is limited.

Be Humble. This character quality is often derided in our society where false pride and "self-inflicted humility" is so common. But considering that humility is the antonym for pride, a man of God would do well to heed the Bible's demand that we put others before ourselves.

Be Devoted. There should never be any question about your complete devotion to God. If the people you serve do not have a clear vision of your surrender to God and your unquestionable dedication to His Word and will, your ministry will not be fruitful.

Be Joyful. Our "joy in the Lord" leads us to praise and thanksgiving for all of His mercies and reminds us that, beyond our earthly happiness, no matter what happens to us, we are heaven-bound which nothing in this world can deny us. It is that unspeakable joy that has always been the triumphant song of martyrs.

Be Prepared. More than the famous Boy Scout slogan, it also applies to other people, including pastors. A pastor does well to be ready and face not just praise and approbation, but criticism and opposition to his ministry. Dwindling church attendance and a drop in giving are not necessarily signs of failure but of God's will to move on to another assignment. A pastorate is never a permanent dwelling place for the minister and his family. Nothing is worse for an ecclesiastical career than to hang on to a pastorate for the often-heard spurious reasons that a child may have to transfer to another school, the wife will have to find another job, or the pastor has made too many friends in town. Be prepared to move on when God calls and know that His will for your life is always better than your own desires.

People have told me repeatedly that the Christian ministry must be the most difficult of all callings. True, it can be. But the servant of God does not cry alone on the battlefield for souls. Our Heavenly Father is always with him and gives him a gloriously unique awareness of His presence, transforming his bitter tears of sorrow into the sweet savor of abundant peace and eternal joy.

Printed in the United States
By Bookmasters